THE
HAPPINESS
STORY

THE
HAPPINESS
STORY

UNLOCKING THE SECRETS
TO LIVING YOUR BEST LIFE

SAVI SHARMA

HarperCollins *Publishers* India

First published in India by HarperCollins *Publishers* 2023
4th Floor, Tower A, Building No. 10, DLF Cyber City,
DLF Phase II, Gurugram, Haryana – 122002
www.harpercollins.co.in

2 4 6 8 10 9 7 5 3 1

P-ISBN: 978-93-5699-552-9
E-ISBN: 978-93-5699-553-6

Typeset in 11.5/15.2 Adobe Garamond at
Manipal Technologies Limited, Manipal

Printed and bound at
Thomson Press (India) Ltd

For Ashvi, my little ray of sunshine, thank you for reminding me every day that true happiness can be found in the simplest moments. You are my greatest source of inspiration. Love you always!

The detailed references pertaining to this book are available on the HarperCollins *Publishers* India website. Scan this QR code to access the same.

Contents

Preface

The pursuit of happiness is the foundation of every human endeavour, whether we realize it or not. It's the fire that ignites our passions and fuels our ambitions, from the first steps we take as children to our last breath as adults. Why is that? Because the original state of the soul is happiness. It is our goal, and it's what we live for. But happiness is a nearly immeasurable emotion: not only is it extremely difficult to gauge but our process of defining it is also likely to be flawed.

Isn't it strange that even after thousands of years, despite our relentless striving, we still find ourselves in a state of misery?

- Why do we feel like we are far away from happiness?
- Why haven't we found the key to ultimate happiness?
- Why do we want happiness?
- What are we missing?

The answer is simple: we've been looking in all the wrong places. Happiness is not just a feeling that comes and goes, it's all about living in a way that makes you content and free from pain and suffering; it means living in a state of bliss and peace, often found in the here and now.

Let me be crystal clear: there's no magic formula for happiness within the pages of this book. I'm sorry to be the one to break it to you, but no such thing exists. My primary aim is to help you focus in the right direction towards happiness.

Let's establish a preeminent point: we often prioritize making others believe we're happy over genuinely vying for our own happiness. This is why the happiness scales are tipped to one side, often leading us to conform to society's standards for what constitutes a happy life. But who cares about what society thinks anyway (when we're doing the right thing, of course)!

Here's the truth: happiness is a choice that comes from within oneself, not from external factors. It doesn't require a perfect life, but rather a willingness to accept imperfections and find joy in the present.

> 'A diamond with a flaw is worth more than a pebble without imperfections.'[1]
>
> Chinese proverb

The good news is there are daily choices we can make to experience the positive effects of happiness. These choices could involve engaging in significant and self-nurturing activities, cultivating a positive outlook, practising forgiveness and compassion, and directing attention towards what we have rather than what we lack. By incorporating these practices into daily life, you can take a step towards cultivating a happier and more fulfilling existence.

So, ask yourself these questions:

- Do you feel happy inside?
- Do you see happiness around you?
- What things are important for you to find happiness?

Now pause for a moment, take a deep breath, and reflect on your answers. Then, join me on a journey of self-discovery as we embark on 'The Happiness Story'. Aristotle taught that happiness comes from good health, wealth, knowledge and friends. Today, through studies based on science, religion and philosophy, we know that only part of this is true.[2] Together, let's unlock the secrets of living a life filled with joy, meaning and purpose.

PART I

THE JOURNEY BEGINS

1

The Fragility of Life

In 2018, my friend died in a car accident. It was devastating; I grieved for months. Years, really. The loss was tragic because she was such a vivacious person—the life of the party. It took me much longer than it should have to realize that I was doing it all wrong. Instead of mourning her death, I should've been honouring her life! After this epiphany, I, along with our mutual friends, visited a couple of orphanages and donated books, bags and food, and celebrated her memory with the little kids. The whole experience was transformative.

Life is fragile, isn't it? One moment we're here, the next we're not. It's as fleeting as a stray balloon: you see it floating away, you almost grasp it, but then it's gone. It can be taken away in the blink of an eye, leaving us to wonder about its meaning and purpose. This is a heavy topic, I know, but it's one we all must come to terms with if we want to live fulfilling lives. As the poet and Sufi mystic Rumi once put it, 'Life is too short to be anything but happy.'[3]

We often get caught up in the busyness of life, forgetting just how delicate it is. We make plans and set goals, but there's no guarantee we'll be around to see them through.

When we finally face the reality of our own mortality, we are forced (against our will) to confront the fact that many of the things we worry about every day are quite trivial. This concept of the fragility of life is a powerful reminder that we should always be mindful of our actions and their consequences.

'We are free to choose our paths, but we can't choose the consequences that come from them.'[4]

Sean Covey

This realization also helps us stay grounded and guides our actions towards benefiting others and ourselves.

Living Intentionally

I like to think of this idea as an opportunity to experience life in detail. I observe the people and things around me; I acknowledge all my feelings, holding on to the positive and letting go of the negative. It seems to me that the negative things in life are of no use to me.

In his 2005 Stanford commencement speech, Steve Jobs said, 'Remembering that I'll be dead soon is the most important tool I've ever encountered to help me make the big choices in life.' These powerful words serve as a reminder that life is fragile and finite, and we should make the most of our time here on earth. So, live it up! *Buy* that yacht! (Just kidding.)

We should aspire to live in such a way that we feel joy rather than fear at the thought that our time is limited. While fear can serve as a survival instinct in certain situations like being alone on a deserted street, in many other circumstances, fear clouds our judgement and often makes things worse than they really are. Like the paralyzing fear of failure that hinders our progress when we think of starting a new creative project, thus preventing us from embracing the joy of exploration and self-expression.

The ultimate goal should be to live a life we can be proud of; one we won't regret. This means being true to ourselves and aligning our actions with our values and beliefs. The *Harvard Business Review* did a study and found that being your true self can be advantageous even at the workplace. Your joy carries over and becomes infectious.[5]

Of course, all this is easier said than done. Getting caught up in the minutiae of daily life and forgetting about the bigger picture is a cakewalk. But by making a conscious effort, we can cultivate this awareness and begin to live more intentionally as our authentic selves.

Here are some tips to put this into practice:

- *Mindfulness Meditation*: According to the Buddha, mindfulness is the path to enlightenment. And we all want to feel enlightened, right? Mindfulness involves bringing your attention to the present moment and accepting it without judgement. By practising mindfulness, you can become more aware of the fleeting nature of life and the importance of cherishing each and every moment.

- *Reflecting on Your Values and Priorities*: What really matters to you? What kind of legacy do you want to leave behind? By answering these questions and living in perfect alignment with your values (almost perfect will do too) you can ensure that you utilize every moment to its fullest.

The Elephant in the Room

Death is a subject that many of us try to avoid thinking about. It's worse than finally getting your kulfi and dropping it on the ground. The sheer thought is a mood killer. But even though we know it's an inevitable part of life, the fear of death often stops us from living our best lives. According to Hindu and Jain scriptures, death is not something to fear. Instead, it's to be thought of as a natural process that is part of the cycle of life. The focus should be on how we *live* our lives.

'The soul is neither born, nor does it die. It has not come into being, does not come into being, and will not come into being. It is unborn, eternal, ever-existing and primaeval.'[6]

Bhagavad Gita

The soul is eternal and unchanging, while the body is just a temporary vessel. We are not just physical forms that will one day wither away and die, we are eternal beings that will continue long after our physical forms have passed. Heady stuff, hmm? But hang on, this is important. The actions we take in our lives, known as karma, determine the fate of the soul in the afterlife. And these breadcrumbs of karma really add up. By freeing ourselves from our karmic bonds, we can achieve liberation or moksha. The word 'liberation' came about in the fifteenth century. Its root is from the Latin *liberātiō*, which translates to 'setting free' or 'release'.[7] Our goal as free people is to set our souls free too.

Our soul is our only constant in life, and it is essential to nurture it. This human life is precious; only we have the mindfulness to think and act in such a way that we can be rid of our karmic worries and let our soul reach its highest potential.

This is why it is crucial to focus on living purposefully and utilizing our time in the best possible manner. We should strive to live in a way that aligns with our beliefs and values, thereby bringing us joy and fulfilment. And I know, striving sounds exhausting, but take a break and drink some water because it's totally worth it in the end.

So, the next time you find yourself getting caught up in the stresses of daily life, take a step back and remind yourself of the bigger picture. Visualize your life on a giant movie screen; no bigger than that. Now, focus. I know it's hard to do up close, but if you take a step back, you'll see everything more clearly. Remember that life is tenuous, and that every moment is a precious opportunity to build good karma, make a positive impact on the world, and cherish the people and experiences that truly matter. Look for what makes you happy and the world a better place, and you will find that they're often the same thing.

2

Self-Awareness

In the post-college phase of my life, a period of perplexity consumed me. Amidst my ongoing chartered accountancy (CA) studies and internship, the future seemed hazy. I stood at the crossroads of survival in this frenetic world, uncertain if the art of wordsmithing (my passion) held the key to my sustenance. Should I tread the well-trodden path, complete my CA and seek employment while reserving my scribblings for stolen moments of leisure? Or should I venture into the enchanting realm of business and become a circus clown? I was completely confounded by all the choices laid out in front of me. I was lost.

Okay, maybe it wasn't quite that dramatic, but it was still frustrating. I knew I wanted to be a writer, but I didn't know how to proceed from that thought. It was a scary notion! How would I get started with the process? How would I even formulate an entire book? I needed to do some serious research and a lot of serious thinking.

Do you also feel lost, confused or unsure about yourself and your life? Do you sometimes wonder who you truly are, what you really want, or what your purpose is in life? Have you ever stopped to think about how much of your life is spent working on autopilot? If the answer is yes, congratulations! You're *human*! Many of us struggle with these questions, and it's okay to feel this way sometimes. The daily routines, habits and patterns we fall into can make us feel like we're not really living at all.

As human beings, we have the unique ability to reflect on our thoughts, feelings and behaviour. Lucky us! This ability to look inward and examine ourselves is what we call 'self-awareness'.

Self-awareness allows us to understand our strengths and weaknesses, our values and beliefs, and our impact on the world around us. It enables us to make conscious decisions and take intentional actions that align with our values and aspirations. Without self-awareness, we would be like ships adrift in the sea, tossed about by the winds and waves of circumstance. And as one of a handful of animals with self-awareness (we share this trait with some primates, dolphins, whales and a few other species), we better use this trait wisely.

What's Stopping You?

I know what you're thinking right now:

- How do I cultivate self-awareness?

- How do I develop this essential skill that will guide me through life's ups and downs?
- I don't even know what I really want or what my values are!

Let me help you. Knowing your true self is a journey that requires self-reflection, introspection and honesty. For most of us, being totally honest with ourselves is a rough road to travel, but don't be afraid!

There are many roadblocks that could hinder the journey towards self-awareness. Here are some of them, followed by tips to help you conquer these obstacles:

- *Fear*: I feel fear. You feel fear. Fear is one of the most common obstacles to self-awareness. While it is debatable whether all animals feel fear, one thing is certain: humans definitely do. The fear of discovering something unpleasant or painful about ourselves can prevent us from looking within. Remember, it's okay to have fears, but we should not let them hold us back. I'm afraid of cockroaches, but I'm not going to let that stop me from scooping one up gently from the floor of my house and placing it back outside. (Where it belongs, I must add.) To overcome our fears, it's helpful to start small and gradually work our way to facing them head on.
- *Denial*: 'Denial is a classic symptom of unhealthy rage', or so the movie *Anger Management* would have us believe.[8] We could be in denial about certain aspects of ourselves or our lives, which could prevent us from seeing

things clearly. To overcome denial, we must be honest with ourselves and open to feedback from others, no matter how difficult and unpleasant it might be to hear.

- *Distractions*: In today's fast-paced world, we are constantly bombarded with distractions that prevent us from focusing on ourselves. It's important to create time and space for self-reflection and introspection, heeding the words of Aristotle: 'Knowing yourself is the beginning of all wisdom.' Meditation, journalling or simply walking in nature are some ways you can introspect.

- *Lack of Self-Compassion*: Often, we are our worst critics. We may judge ourselves harshly and not give ourselves the same compassion and understanding we would give to others. To overcome this roadblock, it's important to practise self-compassion and self-love. This could include positive self-talk, self-care activities or seeking support from loved ones. In 2004, David E. Conroy and Jonathan N. Metzler did an experiment with professional athletes and found that negative self-talk was directly linked to poorer performance.[9] If professional athletes can experience a form of depression due to negative self-talk, we mere mortals will likely fall victim to this hairy monster from time to time too.

- *Attachment to Self-Image*: We often focus too much on the self-image that we want to project to the world, and this can prevent us from being true to ourselves.

To overcome this barrier, we need to let go of the compulsion to please others and instead focus on our own needs and values. That's not to say we're more important than anyone else, but sometimes you must give yourself attention.

By being aware of these roadblocks, and taking steps to overcome them, we can cultivate a greater sense of self-awareness and go on to lead a more fulfilling life.

How to Be More Self-Aware

1. Recognize the Lens Through Which You See the World

'What we see when watching others depends on the clarity of the window through which we look.'[10] That means our thought process and vision have a significant impact on how we interpret the world around us. If we want to change our perception of the world, we need to start by washing our own window.

For example, I used to get so annoyed when my co-workers didn't meet my expectations. But then, one day, I had an epiphany. I realized I was looking at the world through a lens of perfectionism and control. Once I let go of that mindset and embraced compassion and empathy, everything changed. My relationships improved, and I felt a weight lifted off my shoulders. Cleaning that window of mine really paid off!

2. Prioritize Virtues over External Validation

Another important aspect of self-awareness is the recognition that we become what we worship. This means that the things we focus on and prioritize in our lives have a profound impact on who we become. If we constantly prioritize material possessions and external validation, we will become consumed by them. But if we prioritize virtues such as compassion, honesty and gratitude, we will cultivate those qualities within ourselves.

3. Practise Reflection and Self-Improvement

Self-awareness also requires us to be willing to reflect on ourselves and our actions. This means regularly asking ourselves what we lack and how we can improve. It's essential to be realistic, open and honest with ourselves about our strengths and weaknesses, and be willing to ask for help when we need it. True progress and growth come from a willingness to learn and change. Weaknesses are not shameful or signs of failure. They are an opportunity to grow.

'Change is inevitable. Growth is optional.'

John C. Maxwell

One way I practise self-reflection is by journalling. At the end of each day, I write down what went well throughout the day and what I could improve. This helps me stay accountable to myself and ensure that I'm continuously growing and improving. According to psychologists, journalling can considerably reduce symptoms of major depressive disorder, depression and anxiety.[11]

4. Acceptance and Growth

In the realm of youthful camaraderie, where making friends was as easy as snagging the last slice of pizza (a slight exaggeration), I once stumbled upon a wallflower at a friend's birthday party. Being the talkative sort, I decided to befriend this shy one and help her in any way possible. As time passed, her shyness shed its timid cloak, and a radiant confidence emerged. Ah, the missing piece was self-acceptance, tucked away in the dusty corners of her mind like a forgotten treasure. Of course, it wasn't a smooth ride: we encountered obstacles more stubborn than a stubborn vending machine. For instance, she struggled with public speaking, often becoming nervous and anxious when faced with presenting in front of a crowd. However, she tackled this hurdle head on, by actively seeking opportunities to improve her communication skills. She enrolled in public speaking courses, joined a local debate club, and even volunteered to give presentations at college. Through perseverance and practice, she gradually gained the ability to express herself confidently and articulately in front of others.

Accepting ourselves is an important aspect of self-awareness. It means acknowledging our strengths and weaknesses and being okay with who we are. We all have areas where we excel and areas where we struggle. When we accept ourselves the way we are, we can focus on personal growth and become the best version of ourselves.

'The most terrifying thing is to accept oneself completely.'

Carl Jung

Of course, accepting ourselves doesn't mean we shouldn't work on improving our weaknesses. It simply means we don't let our weaknesses define us or hold us back: you're stronger than that! True and lasting happiness comes from the pursuit of virtues and the elimination of our flaws. We're all flawed; the trick is to work on the flaws until we are flawless (or at least hugely improved). It's essential to acknowledge our shortcomings and take active steps towards addressing them. It's also important to remember that growth is a continual process, and we can always be better.

5. Define Your Values

It's essential to establish values for yourself and align your actions with those values. When your values are clear, decisions become easier to make, and actions become more meaningful. Take some time to reflect on what you value most in life and make a conscious effort to live in alignment with that. Keep in mind what Ayn Rand said: 'Happiness is that state of consciousness which proceeds from the achievement of one's values.'

Additionally, it is important to acknowledge that there are limits and a certain sense of decorum to all aspects of life, and it is necessary to respect and follow them. Even minor deviations from your values and established boundaries can have significant consequences over time. Therefore, it is crucial to remain steadfast in upholding your values in all areas of life. This consistency ensures that your actions and choices remain aligned with your core beliefs, promoting a sense of integrity and minimizing potential negative outcomes.

6. Embrace Positive Criticism

For the longest time, I was extremely uncomfortable with criticism (even that given with friendly intentions). I couldn't handle hearing about my defects because I couldn't accept them. One specific instance that stands out is when a close friend provided constructive feedback on my communication style. She highlighted that I often dominated conversations and didn't allow others enough space to express themselves. Though defensive initially, I later chose to embrace the feedback as an opportunity for growth. Through conscious effort and active listening, I improved my ability to connect with others and expanded my knowledge of social behaviour. It surely took some sweat-inducing work, but I came out the other side unscathed. Okay, *relatively* unscathed. However, this experience taught me the value of positive criticism for personal development.

Positive criticism is an essential tool for self-growth. Have the willingness to see your shortcomings and defects. DON'T BE A COWARD. (That came out a little stronger than I intended.) It will help you become a better person.

Seek feedback from trusted friends, family members and mentors who have your best interests at heart. It can be difficult to hear constructive criticism, but it's an invaluable tool for self-improvement.

Self-Awareness + Self-Love = Happiness

Self-awareness is a journey of discovering our true selves—our strengths, weaknesses and desires. It is a powerful tool that enables us to make better decisions and have more fulfilling lives. As you go about your day-to-day life, remember to take the time to reflect and assess how you're feeling, what you're doing, and what impact your actions are having on yourself and those around you. The *Harvard Business Review* filled in the gaps in the oft-accepted definition of 'self-awareness',[12] attesting that when we are truly self-aware, we build better relationships, perform better, are generally happier, run faster, jump higher and even fly. Okay, maybe not the last three I mentioned, but you get the idea. Improvements all around. The study showed that even when we *think* we're self-aware, we're often wrong—so get ready for some mucky introspection.

By understanding our emotions, motivations and values, we can cultivate self-love and acceptance, which leads to greater happiness and inner peace. It's basically the domino effect. (You know, when you stack the dominos, knock one over, and all the others in the line fall in succession.) It's an ongoing process that requires patience, compassion and a willingness to learn and grow. It's going to be a long journey, but if there's one thing humans have shown they're capable of, it is lasting the course. Embrace your unique qualities, be kind to yourself and stay committed to your personal growth journey.

'Between stimulus and response, there is a space. In that space is our power to choose our response. In our response lies our growth and our freedom.'

Viktor Frankl

3

Discovering Your Purpose

I mentioned earlier about not knowing my direction in life initially, and it was an incredibly difficult time. I felt like I had no purpose; there was no meaning in the things I did. I was desperate to do *something* with my life, to make a difference for the immediate world and future generations. It was as if I were walking across quicksand: the harder I tried to move forward, the lesser progress I made.

When I was little, I had always found comfort in the world of words. I could spend hours writing in my diary, contriving intricate stories about this or that, a puppy lost in the forest and rescued by a woodpecker, a trip to Brazil and all the adventures that would take place—you get the drift. I wrote about my family, my friends, my friend's cat, strangers I saw at the market, odd-looking bugs behind my house—the world around me.

When my world was turned upside down and inside out (okay, I am being a bit dramatic, but it did feel that way) during a difficult period of my life, I turned to my true love. Books. I was in my first year of college and swimming in apprehension as I anxiously awaited the results of my CA entrance exams; this was possibly *life*-changing. The ten days I waited for the results were pure torture. So, I decided to return to my familial tradition and shift my focus. In those ten long days, I read somewhere between twelve to fifteen books. Needless to say, I didn't get much sleep.

I was immersed in the images I projected in my mind's eye with every story I read. Even when I *did* sleep, I dreamt of the tales woven by the powerful authors and made up the stories' endings. I already loved books, but it was in those few days that I discovered the transformative power of storytelling. Then, more than ever, I knew I'd found my life's purpose: to touch hearts and inspire readers through my words, which were dripping with positivity, love and hope. This is when my journey began, from short journal entries to the author of bestselling books. This endeavour was fuelled by my passion to paint vivid tales for my readers so their imaginations would light up and leave a positive impact on the world.

As human beings, we all yearn for a sense of purpose and direction. It's a fundamental need that drives us to search for meaning and fulfilment. However, the process of finding your purpose can seem like a daunting, overwhelming task. But you can do it!

As I started writing this chapter, I couldn't help but notice the similarities between the book-writing process and the way we go about finding our purpose in life. Writing a book requires a clear understanding of the book's purpose and audience, while finding our purpose in life requires deep introspection and self-discovery, exploring our passions and values, and discovering what drives us. In reality, what often drives us is the negative. It's human nature to look at the 'I'm here but I really want to be there' mentality. It's not always healthy, though.

In certain situations, negative motivations can be healthy and serve as catalysts for growth and change. For example, dissatisfaction with one's current circumstances can provide the necessary motivation to make positive changes and strive for personal and professional development. Feeling a sense of discomfort or unease with where we are in life can push us to step out of our comfort zones and pursue new opportunities.

However, relying solely on negative motivations can become problematic. Constantly focusing on what we lack or what we want to escape from can lead to a perpetual state of dissatisfaction, anxiety, and unhappiness. It can create a mindset where we are always chasing after external validation or material possessions without finding true fulfilment.

To foster a healthier mindset, it's important to balance negative motivations with positive ones. Positive motivations are those that are rooted in self-improvement, personal growth, and the pursuit of meaningful goals. They involve focusing on what we genuinely desire to achieve rather than what we want to avoid or escape from.

Once we discover our purpose, it's important to incorporate it into everything we do. We need to ensure that every decision we make and every action we take not only aligns with our purpose but furthers it. It is a guiding light that helps us stay on track and navigate life as it waxes and wanes.

Do We Really Need a Purpose?

Absolutely! That's the long and short of it. When I was going through that difficult time after college, I was listless and bored out of my mind. I needed to discover who I was and what I could do for the world. I needed to find my purpose.

You may ask, why is it important to have a purpose in life? My life is going well, can't I just keep living the way I am? Why complicate things? But it's not a complication, really, simply a way of identifying what's truly important to you and what you want to achieve. Once you have a sense of direction, it will be helpful in making decisions that align with your values and goals. When you have a clear purpose, you're more likely to feel fulfilled and satisfied with your life. You must have stopped and asked for directions while travelling at some point or the other. It's the same thing.

Having a purpose can give you a sense of meaning and significance. You will feel like you're contributing to something greater than yourself and making a positive impact on the world. When you have a sense of purpose, you're more likely to feel motivated and engaged in your work and relationships. And you don't feel lost!

How to Find Your Life's Purpose

My lack of direction lasted many years. I constantly felt like I was wandering aimlessly, as if I lacked a clear direction in life—which I did. I was constantly searching for something to give me a sense of purpose. Though I had discovered my passion—writing—it wasn't until I started asking myself some tough questions and reflecting on my experiences that I began to gain clarity on my purpose on earth. After all, as George Eliot said, 'It's never too late to be what you might have been.'

One of the most important things I learnt on my journey was that purpose isn't something you find, it's something you create. It's a culmination of your experiences, passions, talents and values that come together to give you a sense of direction in life. Your purpose may evolve and change over time as you grow and learn more about yourself, but it's something that is always within you. With this evolution, it's important to pick a path; if not, we risk losing ourselves. To tweak a quote from Lewis Carroll's *Alice in Wonderland:* 'If you don't know where you're going, any road will get you there.'

Here are some practical steps to help you:

1. Explore Your Passions

Writing isn't just my livelihood; it's my life. I would be miserable behind a desk in an office job. Thank goodness I changed my mind and left my CA studies! That path wasn't for me.

What are the things that make you feel alive? What do you enjoy doing, even if you don't get paid for it? Start exploring your passions and interests. What we learnt as children was to never be afraid to try new things. Eating spinach and healthy veggies may not have worked out for you, but this will. You never know what might resonate with you and lead you down a new path.

As I just mentioned, I discovered my passion for storytelling during my college days, much to the surprise of people around me. I had originally considered being a journalist or a radio jockey, but I realized that writing books has always been my destiny. Against all odds, I became an author—much to the shock of my high-school English teacher. So, if you're trying to figure out your own path in life, I suggest taking a good hard look at what you're good at and what you love. Who knows, you might just surprise yourself—and everyone else—with your hidden talents!

2. Identify Your Values

What are the things that are important to you? What are the principles that guide your life? For me, it's my family, my writings, my integrity and my spiritual growth. Understanding your values is crucial in finding your purpose because it helps you coordinate your actions with your beliefs. Don't just work for a paycheck. Work for your passion. Studies show that when you love your work, you're more satisfied with life.[13]

One of my core values is honesty, which I learnt from my father. He taught me all about honesty, respect, generosity and a host of other values to complement the lot. They are ingrained in my nature, no different than the ability to read. I believe in being transparent and truthful in all my interactions, and this value guides my actions and decisions in my personal and professional life. That's a good one to start with, but let's move on. There is so much more to discuss!

3. Reflect on Your Impact

From childhood, it was always important for me to have an impact on the world. I wanted to leave my mark on society. Even if I only affected two people, at least I would have helped *somebody*. (Though I hope my work helps a lot more people than that!) What kind of impact do you want to make in the world? What do you want to be remembered for? Reflecting on these questions can help you identify your purpose and the kind of legacy you want to leave behind.

I want to make a positive impact on people's lives through my writing. I want to inspire, educate and empower people through my words, and this purpose drives me to keep writing, even when the going gets tough.

'Don't ask what the world needs. Ask what makes you come alive and go do it. Because what the world needs is people who have come alive.'

Howard Thurman

4. Assess Your Skills and Strengths

Take an inventory of your skills and strengths. What are you naturally good at? What skills have you developed over time? Utilize them by identifying your strengths—*that* can help you find a purpose. Don't be afraid of applying for that job you really want. Who knows, maybe you'll land it! This is one situation where you never want to be pessimistic. Psychological studies have shown that too.[14]

When I was exploring my talent for writing in my school years, I started taking part in various competitions. I discovered that I had a natural ability to express myself through words and communicate complex ideas in a simple yet effective way. I continued to develop my writing skills by reading different books and maintaining constant practice.

'You can only become truly accomplished at something you love … pursue the things you love doing and then do them so well that people can't take their eyes off of you.'

Maya Angelou

5. Find Inspiration in Others

Look to others who have found their purpose and inspiration. Read books, watch videos and seek out mentors who have achieved what you aspire to do. Learn from their experiences and incorporate their lessons into your own journey. If you can't find your tribe in person, take to the internet. There are literally millions of websites with online communities of people who will fan the flames of your curiosity. You just have to scroll through the masses to find others just like you.

While you're going through this metamorphosis, make sure to eliminate the people who stifle your creativity. Focus on what matters to you because it's mental fodder. Everything else is ancillary. To quote Lady Gaga, 'Do not allow people to dim your shine because they are blinded. Tell them to put on some sunglasses, 'cuz we were born this way'!

6. Experiment and Be Open to Change

Ralph Waldo Emerson believed, 'All life is an experiment. The more experiments you make, the better.' Finding your purpose is a journey, not a destination. Be open to experimenting with different ideas and changing course if needed. Whenever you try something new, pause after completing it and see how it made you feel. Are you happy, excited or drained? That feeling will help you decide if you should pursue it or not. Remember that it's okay to make mistakes along the way—it's part of the learning process. Dust yourself off. It's all good.

> 'If you're not making mistakes, then you're not doing anything. I'm positive that a doer makes mistakes.'
>
> John Wooden

I started my career in chartered accountancy. But during the course of my studies, I realized that it wasn't fulfilling my purpose. It was way too far off the path towards my destiny. I had pursued accounting by choice, but then I solidified my love of writing during my free time. I decided to switch gears and focus on writing books to inspire and empower people, and that has been a much better fit for me. I'm four books deep now (this is my fifth), and I'm loving every minute of being a writer.

By following similar steps, you can start to discover your purpose and work towards a more fulfilling life. Remember to stay open to ideas, be patient with yourself, and trust the journey. Life is riddled with possibilities, and you may have an interest in more than one category. (Notice I didn't write, 'You may *excel* in more than one category.')

Stanford researchers did a study on finding the purpose of life, and they discovered that far too many people would focus on only one talent, stifling the possibility that another area of interest may better suit them.[15] Just remember, it's never too late to rethink your chosen purpose if you feel lost or unsure.

Keep Your Purpose in Sight

Discovering your purpose is one thing, the journey towards achieving it is a whole other ball of wax. It can be filled with obstacles and distractions, making it challenging to maintain focus and drive. Staying motivated and committed to your goals requires perseverance, dedication and a willingness to overcome the obstructions blocking your progress.

One thing that helped me was asking myself a simple question before doing anything: 'Will this support the goals I'm trying to achieve?' When we have a clear direction, our priorities naturally shift away from consuming pointless and trivial things, and we can focus on creating something meaningful and fulfilling that brings a greater sense of satisfaction and purpose to our lives. It's a self-fulfilling prophecy.

Here are some tips to help you stay motivated on your journey:

1. Cultivate Discipline for Success

Once my life's direction was decided, I wrote and wrote, but I found it difficult to finish chapters. I could only write my stories when I had sporadic moments of time, and I was *overwhelmed* by the prospect of writing a whole book—an actual story with the whole lives of characters. What I determined I needed to do was create more structure. I needed discipline.

Discipline is the foundation of success. Without discipline, we can easily get distracted by mindless things that do not contribute to our growth at all. To achieve our goals, we need to prioritize what is important to us and eliminate all distractions.

How to Add Discipline to Your Life

- Set clear goals and prioritize them.
- Create a schedule and stick to it.
- Eliminate distractions such as social media and television.
- Stay committed to your goals even when it gets tough.

If you're able to keep yourself from indulging in temporary gratification, you will accomplish what you set out to do. Actually, if you follow *all* of these tips, you'll get there with a smoother ride!

2. Progress from Information to Knowledge

Simply acquiring information is not enough to achieve our goals; we must internalize and believe in the lessons we learn—so that they become a part of us.

Develop a Strong Belief System

- Keep an open mind and be willing to learn.
- Find inspiration in the world around you.
- Meditate or practise mindfulness to strengthen your belief system.
- Surround yourself with people who share your beliefs.
- Study a subject and then use its learnings; that is how you begin to turn information into knowledge.

3. Overcome Your Fears and Ask for What You Want

Sometimes, the hardest thing we need to do is to ask for what we want. Don't let fear or doubt hold you back from asking for what you truly desire in life. Remember, the worst thing that can happen is getting a 'no' in response, but the potential reward is worth the risk. Don't be embarrassed by being turned down: you have to take your shot. Toss that ball into the basket.

Overcome Your Fears

- Visualize success and focus on the positive outcomes of asking for what you want.
- Embrace the discomfort that comes from rejection and use it as an opportunity to grow and learn.
- Remember that rejection is not a reflection of your worth as a person.

4. Step Out of Your Comfort Zone

After Ashvi was born, I fell into a pattern. I would lay in bed or sit in a rocking chair with her, feed her, watch some TV with her and take a nap when she did. I was content; it was a peaceful space. It got to a point where I didn't even want to leave the house. I needed to get up and walk across the border from the comfort zone to a place of progress and pursue the latter.

Your comfort zone is where you grow lazy and forget the opportunities that are out there. I get it; it's all pillowy and warm there. It's safe in your comfort zone, but it's also dangerous to remain there. Make sure you remind yourself to live and not just breathe. You will learn more about yourself and the things that can bring you joy in the world if you go out and experience them.

Challenge Your Brain

- Attempt something new every day.
- Travel to a new place or explore a new hobby.
- Take risks, even if they scare you.
- Push yourself to do something that makes you uncomfortable.

maybe I should work my way out of one comfort zone each day?

According to researchers at Stanford University, stepping out of your comfort zone is the best way to expand your personal growth.[16]

5. Build Meaningful Relationships

I can't take all the credit for my expedition towards progress. My mother and father were really the impetus for me to scramble out of bed, get dressed and go to the park when Ashvi and I went to stay with them. My mother understood, as she has been exactly where I was. She had empathy, while my father, loving as he was, could only have sympathy. It was hard at first, but with a little prodding, I bundled Ashvi up and we went out for a walk. I don't think I could have survived without them.

The people we spend time with can greatly impact our lives. Surround yourself with supportive people who will encourage and motivate you.

Connect Mindfully

- Seek out individuals who share your values and beliefs.
- Be a good listener and offer support to others.
- Prioritize quality over quantity when it comes to relationships.
- Be open and vulnerable with those you trust.

Discovering your purpose is a journey that requires dedication and perseverance, but the rewards are worth the trouble. By living a purposeful life, we can find happiness and contentment in even the smallest moments. It is important to remember that finding our purpose is not a one-time event, it's a continual process of growth and self-discovery. May you find your purpose and, in doing so, discover true happiness.

Self-Study

Exercises

1. Take a five-minute walk outside and focus on the beauty around you. Notice the colours, sounds and smells of nature. Appreciate the vulnerability and beauty of life.
2. Make a list of activities that bring you joy and that you are good at. Choose one activity from the list and spend fifteen minutes doing it every day for a week. Reflect on how it makes you feel and whether it aligns with your sense of purpose.

Journalling Prompts

- Reflect on a time when you experienced loss or had a near-death experience. How did it affect your perspective on life? How can you use this experience to appreciate life more fully?

- Write down three of your greatest strengths and three areas where you would like to improve. How can you leverage your strengths to work on your weaknesses?

- Write about a time when you felt like you were living your purpose. What were you doing? How did it feel? How can you replicate this feeling in your current life?

PART 2

HEALING AND SELF-CARE

1

Healing Your Body

Once I emerged from my comfort zone and started going out more, I decided to make some changes. I resumed going for a run. I went shopping. I got back to my life! It was incredible just how much my body had missed my attention. I decided to *never* let this happen again.

Reconnecting with your body is a continual process. We keep learning more about ourselves. When life gets particularly hectic, we tend to neglect our health—but that's when our bodies need care more than ever. Regularly checking in with the vessel that supports you (and often others as well) will help you connect with your intuition, and guide you on the journey towards a happy and satisfying life.

When I first became a mother, I got so wrapped up in taking care of my infant and getting everything right that I started neglecting my health. I wasn't eating well or often enough, I wasn't exercising, and I rarely saw sunlight. All this took a toll on my health. I fell sick more often, developed digestive problems, and started feeling blue. I'm grateful that I recognized what was going on and was able to rectify it. Well, some of it, anyway. I still wasn't getting enough sleep, but that was unavoidable—babies, am I right? I improved where I could. That's what matters.

Believe me, neglecting your body is not the way to go. Things get a little wonky when you do, and chaos ensues. Our physical and mental health are tremendously intertwined, and we cannot neglect one while expecting the other to flourish. When we fail to take care of our physical body, we increase our chances of conditions like anxiety, anger and fatigue. Who wants that? Not me, that's for sure, and hopefully not you either! Failing to take care of your overall health is basically saying 'I give up!' And you're a trooper. You never surrender.

But don't worry, taking care of your body doesn't have to be a chore (like I was making it). It's all about finding what works for *you*. I found that walking or running outdoors for thirty minutes every day while Ashvi was busy playing with her tutor or grandmother really worked. It helped tremendously. I also adopted a more sattvic diet and embraced my well-being as if my life depended on it. Because it did.

Key Aspects of Physical Health

1. Correct Approach

We all know the two most important factors for good physical health: food and exercise. We know it's necessary to feed our mind to help it grow and improve; the same goes for our physical bodies. The Sage Neuroscience Centre says that when you have a healthy body that gets enough sleep, exercise and healthy food, you're more likely to have fewer digestive issues, a higher threshold for stress, more energy to deal with work or studies, and lesser chances of developing depression.[17] Your body deserves to be fuelled properly and with love.

But here's the thing: a lot of us approach diet and exercise with negative motivations. We try fad diets or ridiculous gym regimes, hoping that changing our appearance will make us happier. We equate health with thinness, as opposed to a state of being that is different for everyone based on their metabolism and genetic makeup.

If you've been in a negative space when it comes to your body, don't worry. You're not alone. It's time to change your mindset from punishment to love.

Being kind to your body might not be an easy thing to do, but it's important to embrace the challenge. It's a rocky road. Building new habits takes practice and effort, just like anything else. Stay on the straight and narrow (for the most part—we all have bad days) and you *will* see results!

'Habits change into character.'

Ovid

And hey, keeping your body strong doesn't mean doing ten chin-ups right away. It means being able to do what you love to do to experience all the important parts of life. Such an approach will make exercise not seem like a chore! Find a way that you enjoy. Take that Zumba class or dance class. Neglecting your body means missing out on happiness. Don't make that mistake!

2. A Good Night's Sleep

Let's talk about something that affects us all—sleep! It's super important for our health and well-being, and it's a chance for our body and mind to recharge. I didn't really sleep much during Ashvi's first year, but that was to be expected. We all know we need seven to nine hours of sleep a night, but did you know that sticking to a regular sleep cycle is just as important?

A study conducted by Harvard University found that these steps could help achieve better sleep:

- Avoid alcohol, caffeine and nicotine.
- Sleep at about the same time every night. Don't deviate too much.
- Create a cosy environment with a comfy mattress.
- Don't do it too close to bedtime, but make exercise a part of your routine.
- Switch off all screens (mobile, computer, TV) at least an hour before bed.
- Limit your beverage consumption at night.
- Don't eat a big meal right before bedtime, but don't go to bed hungry either.[18]

Staying up till the wee hours of the morning or sleeping in until noon won't do your body any favours. There's no such thing as 'catching up' on your sleep. Our bodies work on a natural cycle; if we keep messing with it by staying up too late or sleeping in too much, we're going to feel sluggish all day. Laziness is a form of self-harm, so get up and get moving. Lethargy can even lead to extreme fatigue, memory problems, mood swings and frequent illnesses. No thanks!

3. Healthy Diet

Do you want to feel and function at your best through the day? Well, it all starts with the food you eat! Believe it or not, your diet has a significant impact on your emotional, mental and physical health. Who knew? Once I got serious about eating sattvic foods, everything changed. I was less bloated, more energetic and generally more positive about life.

Now, I understand that the idea of a 'diet' can be daunting, but it doesn't have to be so! Moreover, this isn't dieting; it's a lifestyle change and quite an appetizing (pun intended) one. Healthy eating should come from a place of love and care for your body. Let's ditch the negative labels and restrictions that come with diet culture and focus on incorporating healthy choices into our meals. We are what we eat, as they say.

Keep in mind, eating healthy doesn't mean depriving yourself of the foods you love. It's all about balance and giving your body what it needs to support you in your daily activities. So, listen to your body and fuel it with nourishing foods.

Here are some tips:

- *Start Small*: Don't try to overhaul your entire diet at once. Instead, aim to add one healthy food or recipe to your meals each week.

- *Plan Ahead*: Make a grocery list of healthy foods and plan your meals in advance to ensure you always have healthy options available.

- *Mix It Up*: Try to include fruits and vegetables in every meal, and experiment with different types of healthy proteins and whole grains.

- *Be Mindful*: Take the time to enjoy your food. Eat slowly, really taste every bite, and pay attention to your hunger and fullness cues.

- *Get Creative*: Find healthy alternatives to your favourite not-so-healthy foods. For example, swap out sugary desserts for healthier options like fresh fruit, dark chocolate or homemade fruit sorbet. Yes, you still get to eat chocolate (in smaller quantities).

Sattvic Food

I am sure you have heard of sattvic food. A sattvic diet revolves around eating pure and clean foods that nourish your body and mind. It largely includes items like fresh fruits, vegetables and whole grains. Such a diet helps you feel more centred, grounded and balanced. And guess what? Ayurveda says that sattvic food can balance out the three doshas (energies) in your body: vata, pitta and kapha.

The balance of tridoshas varies from person to person. What works for you might not work for your friend. But this balance depends on your own personal nature, so don't worry too much about it. That's not to say you can't help it progress, though. A sattvic diet is a good place to start.[19]

Sattvic foods are usually light and easy to digest, and they promote clarity, calmness and inner peace. Along with physical and mental growth, they also help with spiritual growth.

So, the next time you feel a bit off-kilter, why not try incorporating some sattvic, healthy, whole foods into your diet? Your body and mind will thank you for it! Bodily praise is what you're looking for in this leg of your transformation.

4. Exercise and Physical Activities

Even though I initially had a hard time going out for daily runs, I eventually began looking forward to this time of the day. I could clear my head and just be free. I even started feeling better mentally. Together with consuming sattvic foods, I felt better than ever with this combination of the two! I never knew that exercise could play such a vital role in everyday wellness. I had to learn it the hard way. You can use my mistakes as a lesson.

Exercise has a bad reputation because it's usually seen only as a way to lose weight, but it's so much more. It is essential for a happier and healthier body, and it should be done with good intentions. In *Your Brain on Exercise*, Gary L. Wenk discusses the benefits of exercise on the brain.[20] Its positive effects register through all your daily activities, even mundane ones like going shopping and making dinner—in essence, everyday things. Having more energy, better brain health and a clearer ability to process thoughts and ideas is what we're aiming for!

Set Small and Attainable Goals

When you start exercising, set small, achievable goals. Don't put yourself through hours of weightlifting if you don't enjoy it. Exercise shouldn't be used as a punishment for over- or undereating. It should come from a place of love, not hate. I emphasize picking an activity you enjoy—yoga, walking, stretching, running, cycling or even dancing (yes, it's a real form of exercise). Anything that elevates your heart rate, gets your blood pumping or makes you a little sweaty counts as exercise.

Exercise Snacks

If you have a busy schedule, don't worry! You don't need to spend hours exercising to reap the benefits. Short bursts of movement throughout the day—also known as 'exercise snacks'—can be just as effective. And I know we all love snacks!

For example, during busy writing days, I take a few ten-minute walks around my office lobby to keep my energy up and my body moving.

The key is to allow whatever movement you choose to work for your lifestyle and schedule. So, let's go, people! We *must* move our bodies with love and intention and enjoy the wealth of benefits that exercise provides.

5. Chronic Pain Management

Living with chronic pain can be incredibly tough, both physically and emotionally. It's important to have a comprehensive treatment plan in place. You can't rely only on medication. This is something I know a thing or two about. In the challenging phase of postpartum, I found myself battling with persistent back pain that cast a shadow over my daily life. It was a constant reminder of the limitations and hardships I faced. But as it's said, don't let pain define you, let it refine you. I needed to take action and here's what I learnt:

- If you're dealing with chronic pain, it's important to work with your healthcare provider to find the right combination of treatments to manage your symptoms. This might include medication, physical therapy or alternative therapies like acupuncture or massage—a multi-pronged attack.

- In addition to these treatments, there are many things you can do on your own to manage chronic pain. Personally, I find that relaxation techniques, like deep breathing and meditation, can be exceptionally helpful. They help reduce stress and tension in your body, which can in turn reduce pain. It's a cycle!

- Exercise is also a great way to manage chronic pain. It might seem counterintuitive to move your body when you're in pain, but gentle exercises like walking, yoga and stretching can actually help reduce pain levels and improve your overall physical and mental health. Pain medications can be addictive, and they can only take you so far. Consider thinking outside the medicine box and finding relief in another, healthier form.

With time, persistence and a comprehensive approach that addresses both the physical and emotional aspects of your pain, you can find ways to manage your symptoms and improve your quality of life. Just be kind to yourself and take it one day at a time.

6. Time in Nature

Let's talk about the great outdoors! Spending time in nature is not just pleasant, it's a tonic for our bodies and minds! We evolve in nature, and our bodies need its elements to function properly. So, make sure you get outside every day and take a deep breath of fresh air, soak up some sunshine, and feel the earth beneath your feet. Go! *Get* that vitamin D.

And the benefits of nature aren't just physical—it can also do wonders for your mental and emotional well-being. There's something about being surrounded by the beauty of nature that makes you feel uplifted. Whether you're hiking in a forest, soaking up some rays at the beach, or sitting under a tree in the park, the healing power of nature is undeniable.

Dr Terry Hartig said, 'There are many reasons why spending time in nature may be good for health and well-being, including getting perspective on life circumstances, reducing stress, and enjoying quality time with friends and family.' Through his study, it was found that the enchanted number is 120 minutes. We need to spend two hours in nature per week. It doesn't have to be all in one shot, either. You can break it up into tiny bite-size pieces over a week.[21]

The best part is, you don't have to go on a vacation or live near a national park to get the benefits of nature. Even just a few minutes outside on your balcony or in a local park can make a big difference. Your body and mind will thank you for it!

7. Relaxation

We connect relaxation only to mental exercise. That is simply not true. Tension can build up in our muscles, causing headaches or back pain, and stress hormones can cause a variety of nasty symptoms.

In today's times, we pack our schedules full of events and put pressure on ourselves to get ahead. While ambition is admirable, it is important for our overall health to schedule time for relaxation and enjoyment. Mahatma Gandhi said, 'There is more to life than increasing its speed.'

Whether it is a session of reflexology or a massage, staying home with a good book, picking up a guitar or a paintbrush, or playing your favourite sport, some 'me time' does everyone good. So tonight, when you sit to work on tomorrow's to-do list, don't forget to allocate some time to just relax. Remember, life is all about balance. So, take care of yourself and see that you unwind and recharge. You're not a workhorse. Go chill, you deserve it!

Building Resilience

Resilience is all about being able to bounce back from tough times, cope with stress and stay positive no matter what life throws your way.

Here are some tips to build resilience:

- Figure out and identify what change you want to bring to your life.
- Excise all negativity—lob it away! People who are negative are much less healthy and happy than those who are positive, and they can bring you down.
- Treat others with kindness. The Dalai Lama XIV urges, 'Be kind whenever possible. It is always possible.'
- Find people who will give you the support you need. After all, as Socrates said, 'A group of donkeys led by a lion can defeat a group of lions led by a donkey.'
- Practise mindfulness and meditation. This helps you stay present in the moment, focus on your breathing and let go of stress and worries.

And don't forget to make time for activities that bring you joy! Quilling, sudoku, exploring, volunteering—whatever it is that makes you happy and helps you relax and recharge.

Taking care of your body is important. It might not always be easy, but with a bit of self-love and persistence, you can make positive changes to your lifestyle that will have a big impact on your overall health and well-being. So, let's commit to taking care of ourselves and living our best lives!

2

Healing Your Mind

~

You know what's categorically important for happiness? Taking care of your mental health! It's easy to focus on external things like work or relationships, but the truth is, our mind plays a huge role in how happy we feel.

Since my struggles with postpartum depression, I've been a fairly happy person. I have bad days, of course, but I do all right. I try to tackle any issue that comes up head on, and never just 'let it go' because it is only coming around to haunt me in the end. I try to take care of my mind as it's all I have to work with.

The mind and body are inextricably connected. That's why taking care of our mental health is super important for our overall happiness and well-being. Even if we're feeling pretty good right now, it's essential to work on mental health so we can handle any challenges that come our way.

In this chapter, we're going to dive into some practical tips and techniques for healing the mind and cultivating a happier, more gratifying life. Let's do this already!

Understanding the Mind

Have you ever wondered about the power of your mind? It's the control centre of all our thoughts, feelings and actions. Our mind determines how we perceive the world around us and how we react to different situations. Most scientists today believe that the mind is like a coin with two sides: the conscious and the subconscious mind.

- The conscious mind is responsible for logical thinking and decision-making.
- The subconscious mind, however, is like an undercover agent that stores all our memories, beliefs and experiences.

It's crucial to understand how our subconscious mind works because it can have a significant impact on our mental health. If we have any negative experiences or beliefs stored in our subconscious, it can affect our day-to-day lives without us even realizing it. Freud called it the 'iceberg theory': there's so much more beneath the surface than is visible. So, it's essential to tackle any negativity in our subconscious and work on improving our mental health. Melt that iceberg. It's the only time global warming is okay—metaphorically speaking.

Common Mental Health Challenges

1. Stress

Stress, a natural response to a perceived threat or challenge, is a common mental health issue that can have a significant impact on our well-being. Fortunately, there are several techniques that we can use to manage stress effectively.

- *Set Boundaries*: Learn to say 'no' to commitments that you don't have time or energy for and prioritize self-care. You must worry about *yourself* sometimes.

- *Take a Mental Health Day*: If you're feeling overwhelmed, take a day off work or other obligations to focus on your mental health. You don't want to risk blowing up at your kids or your colleagues because you didn't listen to your inner self.

- *Identify Your Triggers*: Keep a stress diary to identify the things that trigger your stress. Once you know what they are, you can work on finding ways to manage them. According to an article published in the *Times of India*, a stress diary can be an invaluable tool to manage your stress levels. The one catch is that you must be honest in your writing.[22] If you can't be honest with yourself, who *can* you be honest with?

- *Take a Bath and Pamper Yourself*: A warm bath, a foot massage or a day at the spa can help you relax and relieve tension in your muscles.

- *Laugh*: Laughter is a great stress reliever, so watch a funny movie or TV show (*F.R.I.E.N.D.S.* is my saviour) or spend time with a friend who makes you laugh.
- *Smile*: Studies show that just the act of smiling improves your mental state.

2. Depression

Living with my husband, Ashish, who battles anxiety, panic attacks and depression, has been quite the roller-coaster ride. It's like playing Whack-a-Mole with his emotions, never knowing what mood will pop up next. His struggles, stemming from childhood demons, adult challenges and life's curveballs, have made us approach his condition with utmost seriousness. I try my best to understand what he's going through, but I know I can never fully grasp it from the outside. Nonetheless, I deeply respect his strength as he puts on a smile, plays with our little one, Ashvi, and even lends a helping hand with my work, all while trying his best to find happiness for us all.

Depression is a potentially life-threatening mental health condition that can significantly impact our lives. In simple terms, it is a mood disorder characterized by feelings of sadness, hopelessness and a loss of interest in activities that we typically enjoy.

If you struggle with depression, it's important to seek professional help—therapy, medication or a combination of both. Therapy can help you identify and address the root causes of your mental health challenges, allowing you to develop practical strategies for managing them.

What saved me during postpartum depression:

- *Spending Time Outside*: Natural light and fresh air can help improve your mood.
- *Having a Routine*: Establishing a daily routine will give structure and purpose to your day. According to cognitive behavioural therapist Minal Mahtani, 'Developing a daily routine gives us purpose and a sense of being in control.'[23]
- *Getting Enough Sleep*: Lack of sleep can make depression much worse, so make sure you're getting enough rest each night. It can also make you irritable and no fun to be around.
- *Taking up a New Hobby*: Trying something new can help you feel more engaged and fulfilled. There's nothing more exciting and mentally fulfilling than learning something new—something you have a genuine interest in! When I started painting regularly, I could feel my mood brighten. It was like I could hear the universe's music.
- *Connecting with Others*: Social support is important when dealing with depression, so make an effort to connect with friends and family members. I know, you just don't want to talk to anyone, but it's very important. Just try, okay?
- *Helping others*: Knowing you are making a difference in someone else's life can give you a sense of purpose and

improve your mood. I can't think of anything that makes me happier than knowing I've had a positive impact on someone.

'Wherever you turn, you can find someone who needs you. Even if it is a little thing, do something for which there is no pay but the privilege of doing it. Remember, you don't live in the world all of your own.'

Albert Schweitzer

But let's not forget what it's like to be on the other side of the spectrum, when you have to watch someone you love go through depressive periods. Living with a constantly despondent and downhearted man is no walk in the park. It's like having a constant negative presence living with you: Ashish, Ashvi, me and depression. Ashish does his best to shield Ashvi from the darkness that engulfs him, and we both do what it takes to keep her from being affected, but there are times when the weight of his depression becomes overwhelming. During those moments, I find myself taking care of both him and Ashvi, feeling utterly overwhelmed. That's when self-care and self-love become essential.

To keep my sanity intact, I decided to make walks with Ashvi in her stroller a part of my day. Surprisingly, Ashish began joining us. We established it as a daily routine (though laziness does sneak in occasionally). I feel like we're doing a pretty brilliant job at managing the situation.

If you find yourself living with someone who's battling depression, please remember to make time for self-care. It's your best defence against burning out and falling into the same deep hole. Be part of the solution. Dealing with depression is undoubtedly hard, but taking care of someone with depression is by no means a cakewalk.

3. Nurturing Strong Connections

Social connections are essential for our mental health. Healthy relationships provide us with support, companionship and a sense of belonging. However, building and maintaining healthy relationships can be challenging, especially when we are dealing with mental health issues.

Some tips for maintaining healthy relationships:

- *Communicate Openly and Honestly*: It is essential to have a clear line of communication with our loved ones. We should share our thoughts and feelings with them and listen to their perspectives as well.

- *Set Boundaries*: It is crucial to set healthy boundaries in our relationships. We should let our loved ones know what is and is not acceptable behaviour.

- *Practise Active Listening*: Active listening involves focusing our attention on what the other person is saying and trying to understand their perspective. We should avoid interrupting or dismissing others' feelings and thoughts.

- *Show Appreciation*: It is essential to show our loved ones that we appreciate them. We do this by expressing gratitude, showing affection or doing something kind for them.

- *Seek Support When Needed*: It is okay to ask for support when we need it. We should not hesitate to reach out to our loved ones for help or seek it from a professional if necessary.

4. Cultivating a Positive Outlook

The way we think can significantly impact our mental health. Negative thoughts can lead to stress, anxiety and depression, whereas positive thinking can promote feelings of happiness and well-being. And no, I'm not asking you to be ignorant of the worst-case scenario, just don't fixate on it. Be prepared, but focus on believing that things will work out. Such an outlook will help us deal with difficult situations from a positive standpoint.

Some techniques for cultivating positive thinking:

- *Practise Gratitude*: Let's give a shout-out to gratitude! By focusing on the good things in our lives and showing appreciation for them, we can cultivate a more positive outlook and spread good vibes to those around us. Taking the time to acknowledge and thank the people in our lives not only makes them feel valued, but also boosts our own self-esteem. So why not hop on the gratitude train and spread some joy? It's a total win-win situation!

- *Reframe Negative Thoughts*: Reframing negative thoughts involves taking a negative thought and finding a more positive and realistic perspective. For example, if we are feeling anxious about a presentation, we can reframe our thoughts by focusing on it as an opportunity to learn and grow. That moves us right into our next technique.

- *Bouncing Back*: So you messed up that presentation in your history class. Froze right in the middle of it. Your meeting didn't go very well. The client has opted for another company. It's important that you don't let it weigh you down. You must bounce back and come back even stronger. You *learnt* something. That's what counts. You'll get 'em next time!

[handwritten margin note: Failing at to fail means to live / if you don't fail, you're not living at to fail]

'It is impossible to live without failing at something unless you live so cautiously that you might as well not have lived at all, in which case you have failed by default.'

J.K. Rowling

- *Practise Positive Affirmations*: Practise positive affirmations to boost your mood and promote positive thinking. Choose statements that inspire and resonate with you, then repeat them daily like a mantra. You're in control of your thoughts, so why not make them uplifting and empowering? You can do this!

- *Positive Vibes Only*: The people we surround ourselves with, the places we visit, and the media we consume all have an impact on our mindset. It's a no-brainer—why spend time with Negative Nancys and Debbie Downers when we can surround ourselves with Positive Pattys and Happy Harrys? Let's do some soul-searching and opt for the sunny side of life!

5. Overcoming Anxiety

Anxiety is a feeling of unease, such as worry or fear, that can be mild or severe. It is a natural response to stress and can be useful in some situations. However, when anxiety becomes excessive and interferes with daily life, it becomes a mental health issue. Here are some symptoms:

- You have constant episodes of restlessness.
- An incessant sense of dread or worry follows you around like a puppy.
- You are irritable with the people around you, whether it is deserved or not.
- You are unable to concentrate on anything.
- You find it difficult to sleep.[24]

The good news is there are ways to manage your anxiety:

- *Create a Worry List*: Write down your worries and fears and set aside a specific time each day to address them. Again, honesty is the key.
- *Practise Visualization*: Imagine yourself in a calm, peaceful environment and focus on the details to help you relax.

- *Use Positive Affirmations*: I'll keep saying this until you try for yourself! Repeat positive statements to yourself—such as 'I am calm and in control'—to help you feel more confident and less anxious.

- *Practise Progressive Muscle Relaxation*: Tense and relax different muscle groups in your body to help relieve physical tension and anxiety. Pencil in at least fifteen minutes to do this exercise and be sure you're alone (no distractions).

- *Use Aromatherapy*: Essential oils such as lavender and chamomile can help you relax and reduce anxiety. A meta-analysis was conducted that showed a positive correlation between aromatherapy and pain relief.[25]

6. Addressing Trauma and Grief

Take an inventory of how you're feeling. Don't avoid the emotions you're trying so hard not to think about. Trauma and grief can significantly impact our mental health. They can be paralysing, making it difficult to move on with life. Trauma can cause feelings of anxiety, depression and post-traumatic stress disorder, while grief can cause feelings of sadness and loss. Here are some techniques for coping with trauma and grief:

- *Seek Support*: It is essential to seek support when dealing with trauma or grief. Reach out to loved ones, support groups or mental health professionals.

- *Practise Self-Care*: Self-care techniques can help us manage our emotions, promoting feelings of relaxation and well-being. These can include activities such as meditation, exercise or spending time in nature.

- *Take It One Day at a Time*: Coping with trauma or grief can be challenging, but it is essential to take it one day at a time. We should focus on taking care of ourselves and making small steps towards healing.

Healing the Mind

Taking care of our mental health is crucial for our overall well-being, and it is an ongoing process that requires effort and commitment. By prioritizing our mental health, we can live more fulfilling and meaningful lives. Here are some final thoughts to encourage you to prioritize your mental health:

- *Small Steps Can Make a Big Difference*: To make a significant impact on your mental health, incorporate small habits and practices into your daily routine. Build from there.

- *Take Professional Help*: This is a sign of strength, not weakness. Other people's opinions don't matter! Mental health professionals provide valuable support and guidance in managing challenges.

- *See the Overall Positive Impact*: When we prioritize our mental health, we will improve our relationships, work performance and overall well-being. Investing in our mental health is an investment in all areas of our lives.

- *Be Kind to Yourself*: Practising self-compassion and being kind to yourself is essential in promoting good mental health. Remember to treat yourself with the same kindness and understanding you would offer a friend.

Embrace Acceptance

When I was in my early twenties, I received some not-so-good news about my health; nothing life-threatening, but disheartening nonetheless. Initially, I was upset, but I came to realize that there was a solution. I focused on the positive of the situation, instead of on the 'what ifs' of the future, and everything turned out fine. Had I focused on the here and now at the time, I could have saved myself those days of worry.

Always remember to live in the present. Deepak Chopra put it most succinctly, 'Nothing brings down walls as surely as acceptance.' Being at peace means being in a state of complete acceptance of all that is, right here, right now. This includes accepting ourselves and our circumstances, both good and bad. Acceptance doesn't mean giving up or resigning ourselves to our fate: it means acknowledging the reality of a situation and working towards positive changes. When we embrace acceptance, we can find meaning and purpose in every experience, even the difficult ones.

The Big Picture

Apart from the setback I mentioned previously, I generally try to evaluate a situation before jumping to conclusions. This saves me a lot of time and energy that could be more appropriately spent elsewhere. When life throws you a curveball, it's easy to get side-tracked by the small details and lose sight of the bigger picture. But here's a pro tip: ask yourself if it's worth all the energy you're about to spend on it. Will it matter in the long run? Keeping the bigger picture in mind can help you avoid getting bogged down by the little things and stay focused on your goals and priorities.

It's like the ocean: there are all sorts of creatures swimming around, some of them friendly and others not so much. Either way, I'm still going to flinch when something brushes past my leg in the water. But just like the ocean, our minds can hold both good and bad thoughts and emotions without being pulled in one direction or another. They say being able to have contradictory ideas in your head shows genius. Somebody said it, I'm pretty sure.

Instead of letting external circumstances dictate how we feel, we can take control of our thoughts and feelings. We can choose to focus on the positive and let go of the negative influences that drag us down.

Always remember, you are in charge of your own mind; nobody else. You get to decide what you allow in and what you keep out. By staying focused on what really matters and letting go of the things that don't, you can cultivate a sense of inner peace and strength to help you weather any storm.

'The way I see it, if you want the rainbow, you gotta put up with the rain.'

Dolly Parton

3

Healing Your Heart

‒‒‒‒‒‒

When it comes to healing a broken heart, it's a deeply personal and sometimes tricky journey. But the good news is, you can definitely do it! I've been there myself, and I know how tough it can be to let go of past hurts and move forward. Yet, with a little patience, understanding and a bit of self-love, it's absolutely doable.

One of the most significant roadblocks to healing a broken heart is our tendency to hold on to the past. We get stuck in the negative events that have happened to us and forget about future possibilities—and the future is full of possibilities! It's essential to shift our focus and let go of those negative thoughts and beliefs. Trust me, it's a game-changer!

I'll never forget the pain I felt when a very good friend of mine stopped talking to me. Let's call her Priyanka. When she decided to end our long-time friendship, I was shocked. I knew that we weren't getting along all that well at the moment, but I honestly thought we would work past it. Still, it was like losing a family member. That's what she was.

Family. I retained negative feelings for years, which would emerge not so much as anger, but in my lack of trust in letting anyone be my friend. I didn't let anyone get that close to me again. But then something wonderful happened: I met my husband, Ashish.

He is the most honourable man I know (next to my dad, of course). He is my best friend. But I may never have been willing to let him into my life if I had stayed friends with Priyanka, because I was so disappointed with her uncompromising views that it affected me deeply. To be fair, perhaps I wasn't entirely blameless either, but we were both unwilling to meet the other halfway. The situation got out of hand, and it ended with me not being in the right headspace for any kind of relationship. But it turned out to be happiness that emerged from the pain.

It's also important to remember that healing takes time. There's no quick fix, and it's okay to take as long as you need. Some days it might feel like you're making progress, and other days it might feel like you're taking two steps back. But it's crucial to remember that it's all part of the journey. One of the best things you can do for yourself is take things one step at a time.

'And thus the heart will break, but brokenly live on.'

Lord Byron

How to Heal

1. Let Go of Grudges and Resentment

I only have affectionate memories of my time with Priyanka now. The grudge I had against her was doing me no good, so I let go of it.

Holding on to grudges and resentment can weigh us down and prevent us from moving forward. Forgiveness is not easy, but it's an essential step in healing. It's important to remember that forgiveness doesn't mean forgetting what happened or excusing the behaviour that hurt us. My grandmother used to say, 'I forgive, but I never forget.' According to Dr Karen Schwartz, resentments and grudges can lead to increased heart rate, depression and a basketful of concomitant conditions.[26] Forgiveness is about letting go of the anger and resentment that are holding us back.

From Eknath Easwaran's book on the Bhagavad Gita, 'You will not be punished for your anger, you will be punished by your anger.' Try not to let that anger colour your days. You're better than that.

One way to start the forgiveness process is to try and understand the other person's perspective. This doesn't mean agreeing with their behaviour or condoning it, but just understanding why they acted the way they did. It can also be helpful to talk to someone you trust about how you're feeling and get their perspective.

2. Find Healthy Ways to Cope with Betrayal

When we've been betrayed, it's natural to feel angry and want to seek revenge. We want to hurt the person who hurt us, or at the very least, make them feel the pain we are experiencing. However, revenge is not a healthy or productive way to cope with our emotions. It festers like an untreated wound and perpetuates the cycle of hurt and pain, making it even more difficult to heal. Instead, we can try to find healthier ways to deal with our feelings.

- One way to cope with betrayal is to focus on self-care. This can include activities such as exercise, meditation or spending time with loved ones. (In other words, light exercise for your body and mind.) Finding ways to rebuild trust in ourselves and others is another important aspect of coping with betrayal.

- Building healthy boundaries is a prominent factor in achieving a healthy mind in the first place. If you haven't already done so, now's the time to start. We also need to take time to reflect on our own actions and behaviours and identify any patterns that may have contributed to the betrayal. Enough incidents make a pattern, and patterns add up to intent.

Betrayal is never easy to deal with, but by taking small steps each day and focusing on our own healing and growth, we can move forward with compassion and resilience.

3. Manage Your Guilt

Guilt is a powerful emotion that may consume us if we let it. It can be overwhelming. It's natural to feel guilty when we have made a mistake or hurt someone. It can indicate that you've breached your own code of ethics.

However, holding on to guilt can be toxic and prevent us from moving forward. A little bit of guilt can help you regulate your emotions, stop you from lashing out and make you a great leader. But too much can be a disaster.

Making amends is a powerful way to ease feelings of guilt. If we have hurt someone, it's important to apologize and try to make things right. Even if we can't fix what we've done, we can still take steps to show that we're sorry and we want to do better. This can help us heal ourselves and the people we've hurt.

Much like with depression, it is important to identify our feelings. The nasty little pest that is guilt can feel like something else, such as incompetence, low self-esteem, envy or even resentment.

At the same time, it's also important to forgive ourselves. If we can't forgive ourselves, how can we expect others to do it? We're all human, and we all make mistakes. Learning to forgive ourselves is an important part of healing our hearts and moving on. Healing can involve reframing our thoughts and beliefs about ourselves and focusing on our positive qualities and achievements rather than our mistakes. It is okay to learn from those mistakes and move forward with a renewed sense of purpose and self-awareness.

4. Accept Your Emotion

Dealing with the aftermath of a breakup can be emotionally challenging. It's normal to feel a range of emotions if you're going through one, including sadness, anger and confusion. It can feel like our world has been turned upside down, making it extremely difficult to move forward.

One of the first steps in healing from heartbreak is to allow ourselves to feel and process our emotions. We may feel tempted to numb or avoid uncomfortable feelings, but this will only prolong the pain and adversely affect the healing process. Instead, we should try to be kind and patient with ourselves and give ourselves permission to feel and heal.

Another important aspect of healing from heartbreak is understanding and accepting that it's okay to grieve. The process of grieving is different for everyone, and there's no timeline for it. It's essential to honour our feelings and allow ourselves the time we need to fully repair our hearts and egos. Just remember, don't lose yourself in that phase; you can't stay there forever.

One way to process our emotions is to express them through creative outlets like writing, music or art, or engaging in physical exercise, spending time in nature, practising mindfulness or talking to a therapist or trusted friend. It's essential to find what works best for us and practise self-care regularly. This can help us process our feelings in a healthy way and find some sense of closure.

5. Take Time to Grieve

Losing a loved one can be one of the most difficult experiences we face in life. It can leave us feeling overwhelmed with grief, sadness and a sense of emptiness. Coping with such a loss is a deeply personal experience, and there is no right or wrong way to grieve. It is a process that carries on.

You must try to cope with your grief while still tending to your daily obligations. You need a healthy balance between caring for yourself and caring for others. Too much of either component can knock you off the right path.[27] However, there are some strategies that can help with healing and moving on.

- Allowing ourselves time to grieve. It's important to give ourselves permission to feel the full range of emotions that come with grief; this includes sadness, anger and even guilt. Grieving is a process, and it can take time to come to terms with our loss.

- Finding ways to honour their memory, like I did. This could include creating a memorial or tribute, volunteering for a cause that was important to them, or simply talking about them with others who knew and loved them. By keeping their memory alive, we can find comfort and a sense of connection even in their absence.

- It's also important to seek support from others. This could include friends, family or a support group for those who have experienced a similar loss. Talking about feelings and experiences can help us process our grief and find ways to cope. Don't keep it bottled up inside. It'll turn into a metaphorical ulcer. While we know that actual ulcers are caused by the bacteria H. pylori, recent studies have found that holding in your grief can cause an array of health issues, including heart and immunity problems.

Adhering to these tips won't immediately remove your grief, but they will certainly help you cope with your loss.

6. Express Emotions in a Healthy Way

Understanding and handling emotions in a healthy way is a crucial part of healing a broken heart. It's important to recognize and acknowledge every emotion, whether they are positive or negative, and find ways to manage them in a healthy manner.

- One effective technique is journalling, which can help us process and reflect on our emotions. When my friend died, I started writing in my journal. I wrote absolutely anything that came to mind. It was like free-flow creative writing.

- Another option is therapy, which provides a safe and supportive space to explore our feelings and develop coping strategies. Getting therapy is a sign that you are strong enough to ask for help. It does not mean you are weak!

- It's also important to learn how to express emotions in a healthy way. This means finding ways to communicate feelings without resorting to aggression, manipulation or other harmful behaviours. It can be helpful to practise active listening, which involves giving our full attention to someone else's perspective and validating their feelings. That's not so difficult!

- Additionally, we can learn to use 'I' statements to express our own emotions and needs, rather than blaming or attacking others (such as, 'I feel that you're not listening to me' instead of 'You're not listening to me!').

Finding healthy ways to manage and express our emotions can help us navigate the ups and downs of life with greater ease and resilience. With practice and patience, we can develop a greater sense of emotional balance and inner peace.

7. Activate the Support System

One of the most challenging aspects of healing a broken heart is dealing with feelings of loneliness and isolation. It's important to remember that you don't have to go through this process alone.

Calling on that support system of friends and family can help you feel connected and supported during difficult times. Never allow yourself to feel lonely, because you're not.

- It's important to surround yourself with people who are positive, non-judgemental and who can help us see things from a different perspective. While it can be tempting to isolate yourself, having a support system can help you work through your emotions and find a way forward. And we all want to break through that ice and move forward. What's the alternative, staying in an emotional quagmire? When is that ever a good thing?

- Building strong relationships takes time and effort, but it's worth it. One way to do this is to be vulnerable and honest with the people in our lives. (That was a tough nut to crack for me.) Let them know you need their support. Make time for regular check-ins, whether it's a phone call, text message or in-person visit.

Ben Stein ruminated on this one and said, 'Personal relationships are the fertile soil from which all advancement, all success, all achievement in real life grows.' This can help build trust and deepen our connections with others. It's also important to be a good listener and show empathy towards others. Remember that healing takes time, and it's okay to lean on others for support.

Enduring Pain

Pain and unhappiness are a part of life that we all must face at some point. But we're good at facing stuff, so go forth and crush it. However, it's important to understand that negative emotions don't have to define us. With the right mindset and approach, we can transform our pain into an opportunity for personal growth and resilience.

1. Declutter Your Life and Mind

The first step to finding light in pain and darkness is to declutter. We all accumulate things, relationships and obligations that we don't really need or want. A study conducted by the University of Singapore found that physically decluttering your surroundings can help declutter your mind by making it less scattered and promoting a centred focus.[28]

Things can weigh us down and contribute to feelings of unhappiness, but it's not just things we have to worry about. There's more! The same goes for our thoughts: we often hold on to worries, regrets and fears that prevent us from being fully present in the moment. By decluttering our lives and minds, we can make space for the things that truly matter and focus on what's important. Don't hang on to extra baggage. All it does is pin you down when you're trying to rise.

2. Find Light in the Darkness

Even when we're going through a difficult time, there is always a little light to be found if we look for it. It might be a kind word from a friend, a beautiful sunset or a moment of peace and quiet. Whatever it is, hold on to it and use it to guide you towards a better future. Remember that even the darkest night eventually gives way to dawn. And dawn is a glorious thing.

After I was given the privilege of motherhood, I went through a time when I was suffocated by the wet blanket of postpartum depression. I felt terribly despondent, I had mood swings that I couldn't control, my head and thoughts were foggy, and I had *no* interest in painting or writing or even reading. But worst of all, I had a difficult time bonding with my magical little one, Ashvi.

I was ashamed of my feelings, embarrassed by the whole lot of it. I felt hopeless. This continued for over two months. Then, one day, I woke up and I could see the sun again, feel its warmth on my face and its healing powers. I had some hard work ahead of me, but with the universe by my side, I pushed through. Most importantly, I could hold my baby again without bursting into tears at the sheer terror of being a parent. Since that period of my life concluded, my daughter and I have connected with a love and immense joy that I didn't know was possible. She's two years old now, and we laugh, we play, we go for walks. She is my world, and I wouldn't change a thing.

3. Take Responsibility

We all make mistakes from time to time, but it's important to take responsibility for them. An unspoken rule in our house is that when we make mistakes, we must always evaluate our part in the argument and apologize—and never go to bed angry. Ignoring or brushing off our mistakes will only prolong our pain and prevent us from growing. By acknowledging our mistakes and taking steps to make things right, we can learn from our experiences and become better versions of ourselves.

'It is a painful thing to look at your own trouble and know that you yourself and no one else has made it.'

Sophocles

Final Thoughts

When I was going through postpartum depression, I didn't realize or even acknowledge my feelings. And there were a lot of them. It wasn't until I looked those emotions in the face that I could begin to repair my model of thinking.

- When it comes to healing your heart, it's essential to acknowledge and embrace your emotions rather than fighting or suppressing them. Instead of pushing your feelings away, take the time to understand them and find solutions that work for you.

- Avoid compressing your emotions, as this will only provide temporary relief. Eventually, those repressed feelings will bounce back like a spring and cause further damage. It's like balling up your T-shirt: it may be easier than folding it, but when you do eventually un-ball it, it's full of wrinkles that you now have to figure out how to get rid of. Instead, sit peacefully with your emotions and learn to understand the patterns and triggers that may be causing them.

- By practising self-awareness and mindfulness, you can become more attuned to your emotions and manage them more effectively.

- Cognitive restructuring is another useful strategy that can help you examine negative thoughts and beliefs and challenge them with evidence and logic. It's like magic, but it's actually science.

Remember that healing is a journey that requires patience, self-compassion and a willingness to embrace all your emotions, both positive and negative. The journey may not be easy, but it serves a greater purpose. And don't forget, healing is not linear: setbacks and plateaus are a natural part of the process. But by taking the time to understand and manage your feelings, you can cultivate a greater sense of well-being and experience lasting happiness.

4

Self-Love

If you've spent any time on Twitter or Pinterest (or about a billion other sites), you must've seen a slew of quotes about self-love. Everything from 'You need to love yourself before you can love another' and 'You just need to love yourself more'. You might have rolled your eyes.

What is all the self-love hype about? I love myself, *okay* already. Well, whatever your feelings are about self-love, you must know that loving yourself is the root of all the insane happiness in life. We all deserve a bit of insanity. Seriously, if I had to pick one thing to teach the world about, it would be the concept of self-love—the basis of all love.

I always try to carve out some time for myself. For me, self-love looks like a good cup of coffee or orange juice, paired with an even better book. I like to get all cosy in my chair, with candles or incense burning away (when I feel fancy), and enjoy a quiet, peaceful afternoon while Ashvi takes her nap.

The Trap

First of all, let's clear up some misconceptions: self-love is not just bubble baths, inspirational quotes or a new pair of shoes. Many of these things are the exact opposite of what we really need: to look internally and take care of ourselves. Instead, we fill up our minds and our time with things or people that simply act like duct tape for the larger problem. A lack of self-love will never be outbought or outranked, and it will impact everything we say and do.

As humans, we tend to fall into the comparison trap, which is a massive impediment to self-love. When we scroll social media, mindlessly comparing our lives to others', we end up feeling inferior. We feel less successful or popular than others, and we begin ranking ourselves against other people to see how we stack up.[29]

When we're looking externally at the world and picking ourselves apart, merely reading a self-love quote on our phone will not help. Looking for validation from external sources, buying more things you don't need, and collecting fake friends or artificial relationships will not make you happy. I've been there.

These things are phoney they will not get you closer to happiness because they are rooted in self-hatred. Instead, you must do the inner work that allows you to exude happiness from within, to undoubtedly love yourself regardless of your outside circumstances.

'Self-love is an ocean, and your heart is a vessel. Make it full, and any excess will spill over into the lives of the people you hold dear. But you must come first.'

Beau Taplin

Why Is Self-Love Crucial?

Self-love is the foundation of a happy and fulfilled life. It affects who you date, what you do for work, and who you hang out with. It's all about appreciating yourself—and that appreciation grows when you take action to support your physical, mental and spiritual well-being. Think of it as a plant that needs watering. But self-love isn't just about feeling good. It's about being kind and gentle with yourself, especially when you make mistakes or face challenges.

Instead of beating yourself up, true self-love means seeing these moments as opportunities for growth and improvement. After really looking at my emotions, I don't think I would've found the light again if I hadn't started practising self-love. I started out slow. Five minutes here, ten minutes there; but in the end, I was finally able to reach my goal of up to an hour at a time without feeling guilty. Here's the thing: you need to treat yourself with the same kindness and compassion that you show your loved ones. When you mess up, don't focus on the negative: remind yourself of your worth and your positive qualities. Be your own biggest cheerleader! Pom-poms and all if that's what it takes.

Why is self-love so crucial, you ask? Well, according to *Forbes* magazine, it leads to better self-acceptance, self-esteem, self-forgiveness and self-awareness.[30] And who doesn't want all of those things? So go ahead, love yourself fiercely and unapologetically. You deserve it!

Building Self-Love from Within

Have you ever stopped to listen to the way you talk to yourself? It's time to *start* paying attention. Self-acceptance is the foundation of self-love, so let's start building it up with some positive self-talk. Most adolescents go through a phase when they have a tonne of negative self-talk. ('Nobody likes me!' or 'I'm so ugly.') Unfortunately, that beast can pop up its ugly little head throughout your life if you're not careful.

Be mindful of the voice in your head. No more calling yourself names or making self-deprecating jokes. It's so much more harmful than you think. Your subconscious mind is listening, and it's time to break the pattern of negativity. I fell prey to that in my teens and early twenties. With the stresses and failures of schoolwork and studies and everything, I started on the negative self-talk ('I'm such an idiot', 'Why can't I do anything right?'). But as I grew older, I learnt not to.

Hype yourself up instead of putting yourself down. Cheer for yourself when you mess up. Why? Because you learnt something. You tried. That's what really matters!

Putting the subconscious mind in its place, however, isn't always an easy task. Breaking out of its patterns is hard because it's where our belief system resides. Your beliefs are like the engine powering your car. They give power to your subconscious mind and dictate how you think and feel. If you're running on negativity and bad habits, it's time for a change.

> 'We can lift ourselves, and others as well, when we refuse to remain in the realm of negative thought and cultivate within our hearts an attitude of gratitude.'
>
> Thomas S. Monson

When things really get hard, how do you talk to yourself? Do you truly empower yourself when others can't seem to fit the bill, or do you wallow in the shallow pool of self-pity? Self-pity is akin to defeatism, and we just can't have that for our body or mind.

In order to make the kind of changes you are looking for to really start loving yourself and cultivating self-esteem, you need to get your beliefs and your language on board. It won't be easy to break out of old patterns, but it's worth it. Start fuelling your subconscious mind with positivity and watch yourself grow into the best version of yourself.

A Relationship with Yourself?

To truly start loving yourself, you need to develop a relationship with yourself. You need to take care of your own needs, tend to your own emotions, build yourself up and cheer for yourself when you win. Practising self-love requires you to intimately know yourself and your patterns; the good and the bad. In taking care of my daughter, I get to see every day how she naturally loves herself. No lack of confidence, no questions asked. I've learnt a great deal from my adorable little one. Perhaps one of the greatest lessons.

'If you have the ability to love, love yourself first.'

Charles Bukowski

It's all about knowing your own preferences and tastes, what lights you up and makes you the happiest, what makes you grumpy and what sets your soul on fire. Ask questions of yourself and listen for the answers. They will come.

- Find hobbies that make you feel like a kid again and invest your time and energy in them. (Go play some pickleball!) Loving yourself means encouraging your own hobbies. I love painting (colouring and doodling, if you may) and discovering new cafes. I find it amazing to meet different people and learn about various kinds of brews.

- The purpose of this life is to be the biggest, best and brightest version of yourself. It's imperative that you spend less time worrying about what others think of you, what the cool thing is to do. You're super cool anyway, so *whatever* you do is cool. Give all that energy back to yourself. Put energy into the things that make you the happiest.

- To start living a happier life, you are far better off accepting who you really are than pretending to be someone you're not, or being a people-pleaser.

- Some people may not like you or agree with you, but *it doesn't matter*—the people who love you are the ones who stay. They are the ones who really matter.

- Be brave enough to be your weird, outspoken, freaky-deeky self, and start letting more of the self-love pour in by improving on your shortcomings. None of us is perfect.

Practising Self-Love

Self-love is reinforced and echoed in our internal language, how we think about ourselves and how we talk to ourselves. It can feel hard or even impossible when we notice all the negative thoughts we have about ourselves every day, but remember, practice makes perfect.

When you see negative thoughts or beliefs pop up, correct them lovingly. Rephrase an idea into something more positive and empowering to help get an internal boost. For example, whenever you hear yourself saying, 'I can never do this task', change it to, 'It looks challenging, but I can achieve it with some practice.' My grandmother used to tell me, 'When we really want to, there's nothing we can't achieve.' Some sage advice there!

Self-love is a combination of our beliefs and language, daily habits and rituals, and the bigger things that we do to show gratitude and appreciation to ourselves.

When all these components work together, we will feel love radiating from the inside. Having a solid base of self-love will allow the good things in life to flourish, happiness included. Everything comes back to this. It's an ongoing process that perhaps is the most difficult to master.

Learn how to love yourself and be compassionate towards yourself so you can enjoy a peaceful existence. Remember, we cannot take life so seriously that we forget to really live it.

'The happiness of your life depends on the quality of your thoughts.'

Marcus Aurelius

5

Forgiving Yourself

~

Imagine this: a grand presentation in college, 200 eager faces fixated on me. And what did I do? I had a total meltdown in my head! I stood there, a bewildered doofus under the spotlight, clueless and speechless. The embarrassment haunted me for years, like an annoying ghost that just wouldn't leave. I mean, I've been rocking it since second grade, so what happened to me that day remains a mystery. But here's the deal, my friends: forgiving yourself is a skill worth mastering and seizing. It's the first step towards embracing self-love. So let go of that cringeworthy past like a boss! Dwelling on it won't magically erase that unforgettable moment, trust me.

You cannot truly love yourself when consumed with shame, guilt or suffering from something that happened years or decades ago. Refusal to forgive yourself leads to self-imposed imprisonment. Open your heart to forgiveness and your heart will be open to catch its share of happiness.

Imagine your journey through life as a hike up a mountain. You've got everything you need in your backpack to make it to the top. But you're also carrying some dead weight: your emotional baggage. Let's face it, it's a lot to lug around, even if you've got one of those fancy bags with wheels. So, take a moment to unpack that stuff. You don't need it weighing you down on your journey. Trust me, your shoulders will thank you.

Burden of the Past

Do you want to be a victim of the past, or do you want to create your life from this present moment? Originally, Lao Tzu was credited with saying this, then Junia Bretas, and most recently the hot potato landed on Warren Buffet; whatever the case, this quote just fits, 'If you are depressed, you are living in the past. If you are anxious, you are living in the future. If you are at peace, you are living in the present.'[31] And the present is just peachy.

We are energetic beings, and when you wake up in the morning, your energy is already sapped because some of it is going into feeding the past by reliving it and having such strong negative emotions associated with it. In doing so, you allow the past to affect your present-day emotions.

Think about how much you learn and grow in one year, let alone ten. You are not the same person who made those mistakes in the past. Instead of living in the past, you should be focusing on the moment you're in currently. This will help you live a full life based on how you are feeling right at that moment instead of operating from a place of conditioning or wounds.

Forgiveness

I know it's not easy to let go of the hurt you live with every day, but it isn't serving you any positive purpose. I found that out when I had a fight with my younger brother when we were kids. He and I disagreed on something (I can't even remember what at this point) and we didn't talk for two whole days. It was a lonely two days. We both felt each other's absence and forgave one another without prejudice. We just couldn't take the isolation and being deprived of the camaraderie. Forgiveness is a trait that we all possess, and now it's a trait we must harness.

Staying stuck on the flypaper of past emotions will hold you back from achieving your full expression in this life, so you must forgive those parts of you. You don't need to stay there but, instead, learn the lesson and grow. Holding on to negative emotions or situations will keep you from the fierce love it takes to achieve the peace and happiness we all aspire for.

Give yourself forgiveness for your past and whatever perceived bad thing you may or may not have done; give yourself a break. You are only human! Humans are flawed, imperfect things, no matter how 'perfect' or 'put-together' other people may seem. We have all done something that we're not proud of. Like that one time when I was much younger, and I left my first internship without notice because I really didn't like my boss. Ah, youth.

I'm sure every single person reading this book has felt guilt or shame to some degree at one point or the other. These emotions are normal but constantly dwelling on them is not. Release yourself from the shackles of pain and guilt. Forgive yourself for not knowing better at that time. Forgive yourself for doing the best you could with what was available to you and move on. Doing the best you could is a major accomplishment! Celebrate! Put on some masala chai and throw the confetti in the air.

Steven Colbert reflected on the idea for CNN's Anderson Cooper show, and he said, 'I don't want it to have happened … but if you are grateful for your life … then you have to be grateful for all of it. You can't pick and choose what you're grateful for.'[32]

Steps to Forgiveness

- *Acknowledgement*: The first step to forgiveness is acknowledging and confronting the emotions and memories that have caused you pain. It requires you to identify the source of your hurt and the reasons you feel the way you do. My friend and I had a falling out some years ago. *She* was the source of my hurt. It can be difficult to face these feelings head on, but it's necessary to move forward towards forgiveness.

- *Expressing Yourself:* Now that you have acknowledged the issue, it's time to express all your feelings. Hurt, anger, grudges, negative emotions, whatever you're feeling, express all of them. One study concluded that holding on to grudges really just gives the power over to the other person. In addition, it can contribute to health problems, such as an increased heart rate, obesity and even heart disease.[33] Instead of holding on to it, talk about it out loud, write those feelings down, whatever works best for you. Just pour it out. One thing to remember is that it's okay to feel this way. It's okay to be angry or hurt over what happened.

- *Lessons:* Every experience, good or bad, has a lesson for you to learn and grow. It's essential to recognize what you can learn from your past experiences. Ask yourself what this situation is trying to teach you, what qualities of yours came out because of it, and how it can help you become a better person. Most importantly, how would you feel once you let go of this resentment and accept these new lessons?

- *Gratitude and Compassion:* It's time to show your gratitude, first to the universe for all the situations it put you in and second to yourself for emerging from them strongly and becoming a better person. I know it might sound odd, but being grateful for hard times helps us to be positive and hopeful for the future; it also helps us to be compassionate towards ourselves. It really shows us what we're made of.

Remember, only when we let go of the past can we heal and have a better present and future—because healing starts with forgiveness. And only when we forgive ourselves can we forgive others more easily and heal faster. It's a rather straightforward formula. So take the time to work through your past and learn to let go of any negative emotion. You'll be amazed at how much lighter you feel. Since I forgave my friend, I harbour no ill feelings towards her. I hope she lives a good life.

6
Self-Care

In the midst of life's relentless sandstorms, I cling to my self-care arsenal like a warrior. Head massages, walks and power naps (with my little cuddle partner) are my secret weapons. Amidst being a wife, mom, daughter, writer and content creator, I've learnt that self-care is the missing puzzle piece to feeling complete.

So, let's talk about self-care. It's a buzzword that's been around for a while now, but do we really understand what it means? Many people confuse self-comfort with self-care, but they're not the same thing. Then what exactly is self-care?

Well, it's anything that you do consciously to take care of your mental, emotional and physical health. The trifecta! To truly care for your 'self' you must ask yourself, 'What brings me joy?' then dig deep into that well to find the true answers—nothing superficial. When battling with our mental well-being, keeping track of what makes us feel good serves as a gentle reminder of how to look after ourselves best in times of distress.

Self-Care without Self-Love?

I eventually figured out there was a tiny problem with my approach to healing. I wasn't listening to my inner self. I needed to discover what rejuvenated me. I needed to listen to me. I wasn't allowing myself the ability to self-love, and self-care was only half the equation.

Here's the thing: caring for yourself isn't always rainbows and butterflies. It involves a lot of hard truths and protecting your energy. It's a form of self-love. Without self-love, self-care is kind of pointless.

Even though studies show that 50 per cent of our emotions come from our genetics, the other 50 per cent is learnt behaviour.[34] This includes self-love. Self-love requires you to stop and listen to your internal state of being, then act on what you need, not necessarily what you want. You may wish to indulge in reading a good book in the sunshine on your patio or balcony while sipping an iced latte on a Sunday afternoon because that sounds like luxurious self-care, but are you racked with guilt while doing these things? Always obsessed about what you could be getting done instead? Then there's no point.

Once, a friend of mine—we'll name her Vidhi—told me she was highly stressed and needed some self-care. She asked me to go to a spa with her for the day so she could pamper herself. It sounded lovely, but the only problem was I had some work to finish. I decided to go with her anyway; I wanted to support her because she seemed to be having a tough time. But the entire time Vidhi and I were at the spa, all she did was complain. She complained about her responsibilities, she complained that she didn't have enough time to get things done, and she complained about feeling guilty that she had taken the afternoon off from work! Not exactly what I had pictured from a spa day.

If self-care is done without self-love, it is hardly self-care. Instead of Vidhi taking the afternoon off and truly enjoying it because she felt worthy of taking care of herself, she piled on the self-loathing, which didn't solve anything. Neither she nor I could truly enjoy our time with one another that afternoon, and it ended up causing her more distress than what toiling away at work would have.

The point here is that when you love yourself, you are always listening internally to the things that you need and honouring them. If you are mindful of how you're feeling and thinking in a non-judgemental way, you will be able to honour the things you need without guilt or frustration. Unlike Vidhi, you will be able to listen to yourself and know that taking time away from work will leave you refreshed, with more energy and creative ideas to boot.

But when we fight these impulses and stress about things not getting done, acts of self-care make no difference to our mental state or energy levels. We don't return to work with bright eyes and a positive attitude; we return stressed and feeling like we're already behind.

Ways to Practise Self-Care

Now you know that self-care is an essential aspect of maintaining a healthy and balanced life. It's not just a buzzword; it's a revolutionary act of rebellion against the culture of hustle and burnout. It's a reminder that you are worth taking care of, and you deserve to thrive, not just survive. There are different dimensions of self-care that one can focus on to improve their overall well-being. Here are some examples:

1. Physical Care

Let's face it, neglecting this fine vessel we call our body is like ignoring the maintenance of a luxury sports car and expecting it to perform at its best. Take care of yourself physically, my friend, so you can rock this world with the energy and vitality of a superhero.

- Get a gym routine going.
- Practise yoga and breathing exercises, pranayama.
- Eat nutritious and healthy foods.
- Do stretching exercises.
- Spend time in nature.

2. Emotional Care

Emotions can be wild creatures. But don't let them run amok! Embracing emotional self-care means giving yourself permission to feel, process and heal. So go ahead, indulge in some good, old-fashioned self-compassion and nurture those delicate heartstrings. It's the secret to maintaining your sanity and embracing life's roller coaster with a touch of grace and resilience.

- Engage in slow-paced hobbies such as painting, playing an instrument or journalling. Creative outlets beat emotional burnout.
- Perform acts of kindness for yourself or others. It will make you a happier person.
- Spend quality time with loved ones.
- Express your feelings through writing, talking or simply recording your thoughts on your voice note
- Practise positive affirmations to boost self-confidence. Remember this mantra: a daily dose of self-love keeps the inner critic away.

3. Intellectual Care

Ah, the mind, the magnificent machine of ideas and curiosity. Give it the nourishment it deserves. Engage in intellectual pursuits, stimulate your curiosity and feed your brain with knowledge. After all, a well-fed mind is the key to unlocking endless possibilities and dazzling conversations.

- Read books on topics that interest you: literature, babies, nails, biomechanical engineering—literally anything.
- Learn a new skill or take a course.
- Listen to educational podcasts.
- Seek guidance from a life coach.

4. Sensory Care

Embracing the symphony of sensations that life offers is not just a mere treat; it's a profound act of self-love. When your senses are empowered and vibrant, they become your trusty allies, ready to assist you in conquering anything that comes in your way.

- Create a relaxing atmosphere by lighting candles or incense.
- Take a break from technology and screens.
- Watch a favourite movie or TV show.
- Spend time outdoors in the sun (take your shoes off, feel the earth beneath your toes).
- Get a massage or engage in other forms of physical touch.

5. Spiritual Care

The quest for that deeper connection. Your spirit yearns for nourishment and meaning amidst the chaos of existence. Take time to connect with your inner self, explore your beliefs. When your spirit feels aligned, you'll radiate a serene energy that's simply captivating.

- Practise meditation or mindfulness exercises. Inner peace is the ultimate superpower.
- Pray to a higher power or connect with the universe.

- Read spiritual texts or books.
- Meet with a spiritual teacher or mentor.
- Reaffirm your beliefs and values through daily affirmations or practices.

In a world that glorifies busy-ness and productivity, self-care can feel like a luxury. But the truth is, it's a necessity. Practising self-care is something we all need to make a priority in our lives. And keep in mind, self-care is not a one-size-fits-all thing. It's all about finding what works best for you and what makes you feel good. Whether it's taking a long, luxurious bath, going for a walk or simply saying 'no' to extra commitments. And remember to listen to your needs and prioritize your well-being. You deserve it!

7

Self-Esteem

⌒

Like I wrote earlier, I was outgoing as a twenty-something, but I didn't start out that way. Way before I helped that shy girl at the party (remember her?), I lacked an essential social skill: self-esteem. I was gawky as a kid, and I always compared myself to the other girls in my class. As you can imagine, I never quite measured up in my head. It took years for me to realize the issue, take the reins, and do something about it.

Why do we feel the need to see ourselves from another person's perspective? Why do we look for acceptance and assurance from others? Can't we know our worth in any other way? Maybe by seeing ourselves in the mirror, having eye-to-eye contact with ourselves, and working on things that we don't like. We all have things we don't like to see in ourselves. The more you know and show love to yourself, the more peace you feel inside. It also makes you a lot more confident, ergo, a lot more attractive. And to do so, we need to build high self-esteem.

In simple terms, self-esteem is the way we value and perceive ourselves. Yes, it's our inner voice that determines our worth, how we are as a person. Because nothing is more important than how we feel and think about ourselves. If you want to have better relationships in life, the first one to start with is always the one with yourself. And for that, building self-esteem is a major task. This is not something you can build overnight, though. It takes constant effort. Don't worry, I'm here to help.

Self-Assurance

Do you find yourself seeking approval from friends, family or anyone else? Is it because you want their guidance to improve yourself or because you are always doubtful about your own choices and decisions? When I became a mother I was full of doubt. I didn't know what I was doing. Was I using the right diapers? Was I being a good mother? Can I handle things in a better way? An endless list of self-depreciating questions.

There is a level of self-assurance and self-confidence that we all want to get to. I don't think I'm there yet, but I'm working on it. We all are. It's difficult to be completely self-assured in today's world. All the images we see are of perfect actresses and models who fill us with envy. Dentists urge us to get perfectly straight, pearly-white teeth. Makeup brands vie for our attention, promising that our lives will change if we buy that particular lipstick or blush. But in all that noise, I believe it is possible to find our unique voice by way of self-assurance.

Self-assurance is the key ingredient to building self-esteem. The most potent way to achieve that is by learning to trust yourself. Because when you trust your instincts, you won't need the validation of others to feel confident in your choices. So, let's start believing in ourselves and embracing our inner voice!

Ways to Build Self-Trust

- *Keep Your Promises to Yourself*: When you decide to do something, complete it. Because that will make you trust yourself. And when you trust yourself, you won't seek validation from outside.

- *Define Your Values*: Why do we like someone? Because we admire how they like their life, right? We must do the same for ourselves. Identify your values and take actions that align with them.

- *Boundaries*: Set and maintain boundaries in all your relationships. A lack of boundaries can only lead to resentment and anger. This is especially true with yourself: many times, the most toxic relationship we are in is with ourselves. And it's the hardest one to deal with.

- *Develop Healthy Habits*: We all know the areas where we need improvement: eating right, getting exercise, spending time with family, etc. Consciously work on changing your negative habits to good ones. Go on, eat your veggies, take that spin class, call your mom or just show up.

- *Embrace Change*: We all know the universal fact: 'Change is the only constant.' So, apply this to your growth. Accept when your desires, needs and priorities change over time. Just make sure that the change is in a positive direction.

- *Honour Your Emotions*: We feel different emotions every single day. Happy one minute. Sad the next. Maybe a little excited or nervous? It's important for us to acknowledge and accept them. Ignoring emotions is a very unhealthy practice, a path to more self-harm.

Habits that Cause Low Self-Esteem

- *Procrastination*: I've been guilty of this more than once in my life. I know I have to get those chapters out, but my lil' magic needs to play! I have to organize the cupboards, but I go for a walk instead. I think this is one of the most underrated toxic habits that leads to low self-esteem. When we procrastinate, we keep missing our deadlines and commitments, which in turn makes others and ourselves unhappy and then guilty.

- *Holding on to the Past*: We are all humans, and, as we've established, we are all bound to make mistakes. But the past is for learning and letting go. If we keep lamenting over it and holding grudges, we'll always carry a bag of self-hate, which will keep negating any progress we make.

- *Living in the Comfort Zone*: Prioritizing rest and self-care is one thing, but staying in your comfort zone is another. If we stick to old and familiar ways and don't try anything new, we will not be able to develop confidence and self-worth. Build up your self-confidence; you're worth it. The connection between self-confidence and self-care is real.

- *Comparing Yourself to Others*: When I first had Ashvi, I was concerned that every other mother was doing a better job than me. I was insecure because she was my first baby. And I didn't have the self-confidence to back me up. I forgot that everyone is living their reality and our stories are bound to be different. YOU ARE *YOU*, and nobody else. Get that in your head. Comparing our successes or failures with those of others is never fruitful.

- *Not Having a Purpose*: When we don't have a clear vision of our future, we get stuck at every single step; that is bound to have a negative effect on our self-worth. It makes us feel ineffective, powerless and worthless.

- *Not Taking Ownership*: The victim mentality we carry around with us is the biggest hindrance to building self-esteem. Even though your parents, school bullies, teachers or anybody else may have wronged you and instilled a lack of self-worth in you, it's time to move on. Take responsibility for your life and rebuild what's lacking. A school bully in elementary school teased me for years and made me feel awful. Then I realized the fact that I *let* myself be bullied: I was too timid to stand up for myself. These days I own that experience.

Tips for Improving Self-Esteem

Here comes the good part. Low self-esteem is reversible. You need dedication and some love for yourself. I've already shared one of the most important steps: positive self-talk. Here are some more ways to practise it:

- *Change Your Story*: It wasn't until high school that I started to build my self-confidence. I repeated daily affirmations and started talking to kids I was formerly afraid to approach. Surprise, surprise, it all worked out! Each of us has a narrative we've created about ourselves for years and years; it shapes our self-perception. But we forget to notice that we are growing every day, and with that, our story should also change. Identify all the negative beliefs you have about yourself and challenge them. I like to think that a metaphorical 'duel to the death' is in order, but whatever suits you is fine. You do you. Make conscious efforts to change your narrative and fill it with positive energies and thoughts.

- *Recognize What You're Good At*: Trust me when I say that we all are good at something, whether it's cooking, dancing, drawing, volunteering or being a good friend. And when we do these things, our morale is boosted. Do these things often.

- *Build Positive Relationships*: We have discussed at length how positive relationships play a major role in our lives. If you find that certain people tend to bring you down, try spending less time with them or creating your boundaries around them. Build a fortress. Maybe a moat. With or without alligators. Your choice.

- *Be Kind to Yourself*: I didn't really learn how to be kind to myself until I was a teenager. I started to respect the positive aspects of my personality and excelled in my studies. But whenever I was awkward in public or didn't score well on an exam, I fell into the pit of self-loathing. I scratched and crawled my way out of that habit. Being kind to yourself means being gentle when you feel like criticizing and hating yourself. Criticizing yourself will only lead to low self-esteem. It's a nasty little cycle.

- *Stop Being a People-Pleaser*: Change is necessary in life. But that change should emerge so you can become a better person, not so you can please others. Start saying no when you don't feel comfortable doing something. Say no with conviction. Make them *believe* you. Otherwise, the situations will make you feel overburdened, resentful, angry and sometimes depressed. Be polite but firm.

'The only thing wrong with trying to please everyone is that there's always at least one person who will remain unhappy. You.'

Elizabeth Parker

[handwritten margin note: Be gentle if you feel like criticizing yourself when making a mistake]

- *Give Yourself a Challenge*: It doesn't have to be a big goal. It can be anything you've been waiting to do for a long time. Set a goal and work on accomplishing it. Achieving it will help you increase your self-esteem. Go complete that paper you've been putting off. Take up tight-rope walking. You'll thank yourself.

- *Accept Who You Are*: Yes, you should always strive to be the best version of yourself. Put your best foot forward. But it's also important to accept who and how you are now. Only when you have this acceptance can you wholeheartedly work on improvements.

- *Forgive Yourself*: Still need more convincing on this one? Mistakes are bound to happen when we strive to grow. Keep in mind, you're *still* only human. Leave the divine stuff to God. Stop beating yourself up.

- *Celebrate the Little Things*: Now this is sorcery (not really). Celebrating small victories is a great way to build self-confidence and feel better about yourself, and that in turn helps you achieve the bigger and more important stuff in life. Hey! You remembered to floss every night, kudos!

I hope you found some useful tips and insights to help you feel more confident and positive about yourself. Remember, building self-esteem takes time and effort, but it's totally worth it. Keep practising self-compassion, challenging negative self-talk and focusing on your strengths. And if you ever need a boost, don't hesitate to reach out to someone you trust or even a professional.

You've got this! Go forth!

'We are what our thoughts have made us; so, take care about what you think. Words are secondary. Thoughts live; they travel far.'

Swami Vivekananda

Self-Study

Exercises

1. Try a new physical activity, such as yoga or dancing, for one week, and notice how it affects your body.
2. Practise mindfulness meditation for ten to fifteen minutes each day.
3. Write down your negative thoughts and then challenge them with positive affirmations.
4. Write a letter to someone who has hurt you (even if you don't send it).
5. Practise self-forgiveness by acknowledging your mistakes and offering yourself compassion.

Journalling Prompts

- How does your body feel when you are stressed or anxious? What can you do to reduce those feelings?
- What are some of your most common negative thoughts? How do you think they affect you on a daily basis?
- What are some of the most painful experiences you've had? How have they affected you?
- What are some ways you can show yourself compassion and kindness?
- What negative thoughts do you have about yourself? How do you think you can replace them with positive ones?
- Reflect on how you've grown and learnt from mistakes.
- What are some of your strengths and accomplishments, both big and small?

PART 3

LIVING A MINDFUL LIFESTYLE

1

Daily Mindful Routine

Do you ever feel like you're going through the motions of life in a robotic fashion, without really being present in the moment? It's easy to get caught up in the stress and chaos of daily life, but it doesn't have to be that way. By incorporating mindfulness into your regular routine, you can make a huge difference in how you experience life. *New York Times* bestselling author and expert in the practices of meditation and mindfulness Sharon Salzburg reminds us, 'Mindfulness isn't difficult, we just need to remember to do it.'

I'm quite sure I'd be lost in a sea of chaos and calamity without my mindfulness routine. I strive to be fully present in every moment, whether I'm stuck in traffic or scrubbing my daughter's beloved toys. Balancing the demands of motherhood, writing and personal commitments has taught me the art of effective time management. I meticulously plan my days, assigning dedicated blocks of time to each responsibility.

But let's be real here, even the most zen-like beings mess up sometimes. Getting back into that tranquil zone can be a challenge. Nevertheless, I stay determined to find my way back to the land of zen, one mindful step at a time. After all, what's life without a touch of adventure on the path to daily mindfulness?

Mindfulness is all about being aware, in the here and now, acknowledging what you are doing, thinking and feeling in this very second. It's not about trying to get rid of your thoughts or emotions, but rather about recognizing them and letting them pass by without judgement. By doing so, you can experience more joy, peace and happiness. Studies show that mindfulness reduces stress and all its sidekicks and makes you more aware of events like sugar crashes after eating sweets, or the endorphin rush you get after exercising. Understanding those effects can help you practise better habits.[35]

'I don't want to be at the mercy of my emotions. I want to use them, to enjoy them, and to dominate them.'

Oscar Wilde

One way to start leading a mindful life is by implementing proper morning and night routines. This helps you set the tone for the day ahead and wind down at night. But why should you bother with mindfulness? I'll *tell* you why!

- *Knowing Yourself Better*: When you are present in the moment, you become more aware of yourself. The whole self, your thoughts, feelings and actions. This self-awareness helps you to understand yourself better, which can lead to personal growth and development.

- *Enhancing Physical and Mental Health*: Studies have shown that mindfulness can reduce symptoms of depression and anxiety, and even lower blood pressure and improve immunity.

- *Reducing Overthinking and Procrastination*: When you are present in the moment, you are less likely to get lost in your thoughts and more likely to act. Let's work on keeping your mind from wandering off to the high-school farewell dance where you slow-danced with that really cute guy whose name you'll never forget.

- *Improving Concentration*: Mindfulness helps you focus your attention and stay present, which can improve your productivity and concentration. Even if you're doing something as mundane as washing dishes, do it the best way possible by being fully present.

- *Reducing Anxiety and Stress*: Mindfulness can help you manage your thoughts and emotions more effectively, reducing anxiety and stress.

- *Bringing Bad Habits to Your Attention*: Mindfulness helps you become more aware of your habits and behaviours, allowing you to make positive changes. I feel like we should always be aware of our habits and behaviours. It's a good habit!

- *Developing Resilience*: When you practise mindfulness, you become better equipped to handle life's challenges and setbacks. You got a flat tyre? So what? Take a deep

Resilience from mindfulness makes life's inevitable challenges easier to deal with breath and calmly find a solution. Missed a deadline? Regroup, make a plan, and move forward. Faced with criticism? Use it as an opportunity to learn and grow.

- *Leading to a Happier Life*: Ultimately, mindfulness can help you live a happier and more fulfilling life by bringing greater awareness, joy and peace to your daily experiences.

Starting the Day with Mindfulness

Let me be honest: mornings are tough for me, and maybe for you too. Maybe you're a busy parent, you're still in school or college, or you have a demanding job that requires your attention in the early hours. That doesn't mean you can't infuse some mindfulness into your mornings.

I have both a child and an early-morning job. My daughter *is* my early-morning job. She wakes me up at 6 a.m., an hour at which I'm just not functional. Don't get me wrong, I love my daughter with every fibre of my being. But I have to meditate and practise mindfulness to keep from operating on autopilot mode.

Let me share a very simple way to introduce you to this beautiful practice of mindfulness with a few easy steps.

How to Start the Day Mindfully

- First things first. Sit on your bed and take a few deep breaths and welcome the day. Say your morning prayers if you like.

- Make your bed and head to the bathroom. After freshening up, you can change your outfit—if you feel lazy in your pyjamas—to feel fresh and energetic. This is especially true for those of us who work from home. I fell into a pyjama phase once. It's not easy to get your way out of that one.

- Set your intention for the day. Let this be your guiding light that helps you make decisions every day, based on what you need. Example: Today I'll be kind to others and myself; I will be patient with others; I will stay grounded; and I will eat mindfully.

- Drink a glass of warm water, focusing on every sip.

- Read a non-fiction book for thirty minutes. Not only will you gain knowledge about yourself, but you'll also learn from the mistakes and triumphs of others. And the best part? You can pick up tips and tricks to improve those parts of your life that need a little extra TLC. It will help you be a *better* you![36]

- Work out. You know this one! Just move your body in whatever way you feel comfortable. Go for runs, do some cardio, hit the gym or practise yoga and meditation.

- Always allocate time for breakfast. It is the most important meal of your day so treat it as one. It has been found that those who eat breakfast regularly eat fewer calories and healthier foods throughout the day.[37]

- Check your to-do list and get going with the most important task of the day.

And *bam*! You rocked your morning! The rest of the day will surely be just as great.

Unwind and Recharge

My end-of-the-day ritual includes reading, putting my daughter to bed, brushing my teeth, washing my face, doing some gentle stretching, and going to bed. But my absolute favourite way to unwind is rocking my daughter to sleep. There's something special about it. It's not just that I'm holding a tiny person, my own flesh and blood, in my arms; it's the rhythm of rocking back and forth that washes away the morsels of my day. Tomorrow, I'll start anew.

The end of the day is just as important as the beginning. A mindful nightly ritual can help you wind down and prepare your body and mind for a restful sleep. It's the perfect time to reflect on the day that has passed, let go of any stress and negativity, and prepare your mind and body before you start counting sheep.

Simple Practices to Make a Big Difference

- Read a feel-good book for thirty minutes. Reading shifts your attention from the day's stress and eases your mind, helps you with insomnia and reduces stress. What's more, according to a Berkeley University study, the consensus is that reading fiction can boost your compassion and empathy, while making you more capable of seeing other people's points of view.[38] We're working on all of that anyway. Why not give it a whirl?

- Stretch. After all the hustle-bustle of the day, your body is bound to be tense—even if you don't realize it. Add a five-minute stretch routine to loosen up your body, relieve stress and feel relaxed. You can try these basic exercises: happy-baby pose; neck, shoulder and feet stretches; and the seated-forward bend.

- Wash your face and brush your teeth.

- Wear fresh, comfortable nightwear. It'll enhance the positive vibes.

- Set goals for the next day. I know every morning brings its own plans, but having a list of to-dos can help when you wake up because you know what to expect from the day.

- Journal. No need to dust off your Booker Prize for this one. Just as you write your social media captions, write down whatever is going through your mind about the day, whatever made you happy, sad, angry—anything, really. Pour it out before hitting the bed.

- Write down three things you are grateful for.

- Shut down your social media sites at least an hour before you hit the bed. Trust me, your FOMO is completely unwarranted. Nothing important will be missed.

- Some more things you can try to make your sleep better and more relaxed are aroma diffusers to create a soothing atmosphere, drops of lavender oil on your pillow and lulling music. I prefer spiritual songs, but you can try rain sounds, white noise or even specific sleep music. It's cool to feel like you're falling asleep in a rainforest.

Remember, mindfulness doesn't have to be a daunting task that takes up hours of your day. It can be as simple as taking a few moments to appreciate the beauty around you or being present in your daily tasks—be it holding your baby, running errands or crunching numbers. Eventually, it will fit like an old glove so much so that you won't even realize you're doing it. With mindfulness, you can find peace in the midst of chaos and joy in the simplest moments. So go ahead and take that first step; you never know where it might lead you!

'The fruit of mindfulness practice is the realization that peace and joy are available within us and around us, right here and right now.'

Thich Nhat Hanh

2

Time Management

I'm a mom. I'm a wife. I'm a writer. And I'm me. How am I supposed to tend to all those characters in one day? Sometimes, life gets so busy that I end up neglecting all those roles while drowning in errands and other commitments.

Tick-tock, tick-tock, goes the clock. Time is a precious commodity, and once it's gone, it's gone for good. So, ask yourself, 'Am I using my time wisely?' Or are you squandering it away on things that don't really matter? It's time to take charge and manage it like a boss. Don't let the YOLO mindset make you waste time on unnecessary activities.

To get a grip on time management, start by identifying the culprits that steal your precious hours.

- *Procrastination*: The granddaddy of all timewasters.
- *Social Media*: It lures you in with mindless scrolling, and before you know it, hours have vanished.
- *Not Having a Physical To-Do List*: Relying on memory is not the best option in this world of distractions. How many times do you walk into the kitchen and

not remember why you're there? Yeah, think about it. Memory is a little trickster.

- *Not Planning*: Spontaneity is fun, but not when it derails your productivity.
- *Being Messy*: Clear out your closet and your mind.
- *Unrealistic Goals*: Like my professor once told me, your goals must be SMART.

Specific–Measurable–Attainable–Relevant–Timebound.

Now that you know what's holding you back, take control of your time. Prioritize what matters, and let the clock work for you, not against you.

Procrastination

We've all danced with this devil at some point, delaying the inevitable and opting for the easier, less important task. But why do we succumb to this self-sabotage? While poor time management and lack of discipline can play a role, there's often a deeper cause. Make no mistake, procrastination isn't laziness; it's a conscious decision to avoid what we should be doing.

Confession time. I was once a world-class procrastinator extraordinaire. In high school, I had perfected the art of postponing projects and homework until the eleventh hour. Sure, I managed to turn everything in on time (almost always), but let's just say it wasn't a phase I'm proud of.

Don't get me wrong, I was still a stellar student. I just had a knack for embracing the last-minute frenzy of finishing a task. Perhaps it was the thrill of knowing I could procrastinate and still come out unscathed. Or maybe, deep down, I was simply too cool for homework, already a master of the material. Ah, the joys of academic mischief!

However harmless it may seem in the moment, it can have dire consequences down the line. Even small bouts of procrastination can lead to guilt, decreased productivity and a sense of dissatisfaction with work. And if we let it go on for too long, we risk plummeting into a dark pit of anxiety, stress, depression, insomnia and a whole host of health issues. So let's not make excuses for procrastination. Kick it to the curb and start tackling those tasks head on.

Common Reasons for Procrastination and Time Mismanagement

1. Lack of Motivation

It may be my passion, but there have been times when I incontrovertibly did not feel like writing—even with a giant deadline looming and a basketful of storytelling to do. Maybe it was a gorgeous day and I felt like going to the beach instead.

There are many times when, for one reason or another, we simply don't want to do a particular job. Maybe we're tired. Maybe the job bores us. Maybe we feel overwhelmed. For whatever reason, we feel a distinct lack of motivation and thus procrastinate indefinitely. No gumption, no productivity.

2. Abstract Objectives

Another common reason for procrastination is that our objective for doing something is abstract and unclear. For example, a goal of reading more books or walking regularly every day is relatively abstract. On the other hand, the goal of reading one book per fortnight or walking 10,000 steps every day is much more concrete and achievable. Now that we have a strategy, we can charge ahead.

3. Lack of Instant Gratification

Unfortunately, most of us struggle to appreciate and anticipate rewards that will be achieved in the future. In other words, if we know we won't reap the benefits of a particular action for a long time, we are much less likely to want to perform that action. This, in turn, leads to more procrastination. It's a cycle inside the cycle of procrastination inside the cycle of life. Get it?

4. Feeling Overwhelmed

Sometimes, we have so many options in front of us that we become paralysed, unable to make any meaningful choices. It's called analysis paralysis—when you have so many decisions or choices in front of you that you can't pick one. This is especially relevant if the choices are one amongst dozens; for instance, when deciding which car to buy.[39]

5. Anxiety and Fear

If a particular task makes you anxious, there's a good chance you'll procrastinate on it. When we have an important call to make or an email to send, we become anxious about how to give our best, and that leads to procrastination. Anxiety and fear are often in line with my next point.

6. Fear of Failure

No one likes to fail at anything. When we have several tasks at hand at which we can fail, we try to avoid them till the very last moment. But remember the words of American author Elbert Hubbard: 'There is no failure except in no longer trying.'

Tools to Help You Manage Your Time Better

I used to have trouble managing all the roles I had to fill. I was new at some of them, and I didn't have the drill down pat yet. It took me an ocean of research, but I finally found some ways to help me to stay on track throughout the day. I know it may seem impossible to break this habit, but with these simple changes—and some tough ones tossed into the mix—we can become better at handling work and life. If I can, so can you!

- Start with finishing the toughest tasks of the day first. I know it's tempting to put them off but doing them early will give you more time and energy to focus while you're bright-eyed and bushy-tailed, resulting in better quality work.

- Get rid of distractions and focus on one thing at a time. Multitasking may seem efficient, but it actually obliterates your concentration levels and quality of work.

- Manage your inbox and unsubscribe from useless updates. Turning off email updates will also help you stay more focused. There's nothing more annoying when you're trying to concentrate than the constant *DING* of notifications on your phone or computer.

- Set deadlines and stick to them. This will help you prioritize tasks and plan your day accordingly.

- Use a calendar, diary or notepad to keep track of your tasks. Having a plan in place will allow you to adjust it as needed. The *Harvard Business Review* suggests setting specific times for each task or deadline. Try using the to-do app on your phone, or make a list, but only focus on one thing per day. If you get more accomplished, great! But even if you only get that one thing done, you'll know you did it really well.

- Take short breaks after working for an hour to keep your mind fresh and avoid burnout. *Forbes* magazine says, 'You can't expect to run on 100% if you don't give yourself the time you need to rejuvenate yourself and feel ready to return to your tasks.'

- Leave some empty slots in your day. You don't have to do everything in one day, and having some free time will help you feel more peaceful.

- Keep your workspace neat and tidy. This will increase your productivity and help you feel more energized through the day. Who doesn't like a clean, organized house? It makes you feel better. It's the same idea.

- Remember, it's critical to cut out the things that you *don't* need to focus on so you can focus on what really matters. You must figure out what's most essential to you.
- Delegate tasks when possible so you can direct your attention to more important things. Don't be afraid to ask for help when you need it!

I hope you found these tips and strategies useful and applicable to your daily life. Remember, effective time management is not about being perfect or achieving an unrealistic level of productivity. It's about finding a balance that works for you without sacrificing your well-being. With practice, patience and persistence (let's call them the three Ps of productivity), you'll be surprised at how much you can accomplish and how much time you can save for the things that matter most.

'A plan is what, a schedule is when. It takes both a plan and a schedule to get things done.'

Peter Turla

3
Gratitude

~

Gratitude has become a much-used word these days, and for a very good reason! You don't need a reason to be grateful, but here are a few ideas to drive home its importance. Gratitude doesn't mean merely saying thank you for the things you have. It means acknowledging the goodness in your life, embracing it and being thankful to the source of it from the core of your very being.

Why Be Grateful?

Well, in this fast-paced, competitive environment, we tend to notice and worry about what our lives are lacking. Because of our drive to succeed and achieve everything, we focus on what stands in our way. We tend to tune in to the things we don't have—diamonds, a flat tummy, the CEO rank, money, a perfect relationship, the newest flat-screen 5K TV. But when this is how we view the world, we measure our worth by deficits rather than successes. That can make us feel downright crummy!

Feelings of inadequacy, imperfection and envy are barriers to happiness. When we harbour these feelings, we limit our capacity to feel happy and fulfilled. Although we often strive to find happiness by trying to achieve the greatest of things, this approach holds us back.

A Shift in Mindset

That's where gratitude comes in. It's the practice of noticing and appreciating what we *already* have that can bring more happiness. Feeling grateful for what's going well in our lives has a remarkable impact on how we feel about ourselves and the world around us.

Showing gratitude is one of the simplest things we can do for ourselves and each other, and guess what? It's completely free! Free stuff rocks. Wait, it gets better. It's not something where you either have it in you or you don't. Sure, some people are naturally predisposed to showcase appreciation for everything and everyone in their lives; it comes easily to them. But being grateful and expressing gratitude is a state of mind that we can all develop with a little practice.

If you don't already feel like you are enough, keep reading!

'Gratitude turns what we have into enough.'

Melody Beattie

How Gratitude Helps Us

1. Shift in Focus

No matter how low I get or how unlucky I feel, I know things will only get better. I jumped into the slowest queue in the store. I caught every red traffic signal during a fifty-mile ride. So what? Tomorrow will be better!

There are times when nothing seems to be working in our favour and everything is going down in flames, leaving us disheartened and distraught. But by deliberately looking at the good in any given scenario, we shift our focus from the bad to the good, which gives us some hope and makes it easier to deal with the situation at hand in the correct way. Stuck at a series of red traffic signals? Think of it as a time to take some deep breaths. Or an opportunity to practise mindfulness.

> 'Reality is created by the mind; we can change our reality by changing our mind.'
>
> Plato

2. Makes Us Happier

I was raised to love and respect our families unconditionally, and now Ashvi will carry on the tradition. When we take the time to acknowledge and give thanks for the love and goodness that we already have, we attract more people and situations which, in turn, fill us with more love and happiness! That's quite the chain reaction! It turns out that noticing what we already have can make us feel more positive about our lives.

3. Reduces Materialism

One idea we've been schooling our li'l magic in since she was an infant is to give thanks for whatever she has. We haven't let her have too many toys, and it hasn't affected her in any way. She's surrounded by heaps of love from our entire family, and she loves us back. She's a happy, healthy little girl who wants for nothing because she's grateful for what she has.

Unsurprisingly, those who are grateful also tend to be less materialistic because people who appreciate what they already have are less likely to focus on obtaining more. We probably don't need [insert item] anyway.

I've never been a particularly materialistic person. My father raised me to be happy with what I had because there are millions of people who didn't have the luxuries that I had been afforded (like art lessons). He had learnt it from his father who learnt it from his father and so on. I'm prouder of him than any person I've ever known. To this day, I still do not go out and buy the latest models of phones or clothes. I'm satisfied with my life.

4. Improves Relationships

Showing gratitude to loved ones is a great way to make them feel good and make *ourselves* feel good in the process, which will make the relationship all the better. Those who communicate their gratitude to their family, friends, and partners are more likely to work through problems and concerns, giving way to a more positive perception of their relationship.

5. Improves Health

I'm very grateful for the people and things in my life. I appreciate the comforting home I share, the work I do, my family and everything under the sun. Being grateful positively impacts our mental and physical health. It strengthens our immune system, improves our duration and quality of sleep, and reduces levels of anxiety and depression. And people who exercise more gratitude also tend to their health needs more eagerly; in doing so, they can help prevent ailments from happening in the first place. It's a different kind of exercise, but it's still exercise.

6. Benevolent Nature

My parents raised me to be grateful for what I have, and Ashvi only solidified these values with wide-eyed wonder instead of boredom with her few toys. By practising gratitude, we realize how much we receive from others—be it our family, friends, society or the universe, and that helps us control our self-centredness. With that, we become more giving and try to help everyone we can in all possible ways. Researchers at the University of Chicago have all but validated this theory by finding an association between loneliness and self-centredness. They saw that, in many cases, self-centredness can be avoided or remedied by having closer relationships with friends and family. Self-centredness is linked with egocentrism, materialism and a lack of modesty.[40] Let's face it, modesty is in vogue.

Ways to Practice Gratitude Daily

1. Gratitude Journal

I suppose this is the easiest way to kick-start this new habit as you don't have to involve or interact with anyone else to do it. Pick up a diary and pen and write down the things you're grateful for. It can be as simple as your morning coffee, a hot shower after a long day at work, having the most loving family and friends, having enough food and good health, completing a project, buying your dream car or getting the job you wanted. As you progress, you may also try writing about the whys. When you focus on *why* you're grateful for something and how your life would be different without it, you value it even more. Like coffee—I would be a grumpy killjoy without my daily cuppa.

2. Appreciate Even the Small Wins

Gratitude doesn't *have* to be saved for the 'big' things in life. The habit of being grateful starts with appreciating every good thing in life and recognizing that there is nothing too small for you to be thankful for. Even if it is as simple as a perfect sunny morning or the early delivery of your order, be thankful.

'He is a wise man who does not grieve for the things which he has not but rejoices for those which he has.'

Epictetus

3. Practise Mindfulness

I always try to use fifteen minutes in the morning to think of what I appreciate in my life and then to practise a few asanas if I have time.

Sit down in a comfortable position every evening or morning (or both—go for the gold!) and think about five to seven things you are grateful for. The trick is that you need to visualize it in your mind and stay with that energy of gratitude, feeling it in your body. I visualize my family, my child and my life. I don't mean to imply that everything is perfect, but it's mine. Doing this every day will rewire your brain to be naturally more grateful. And you'll see, you're going to start feeling happier day by day.

4. Compliment Someone

A simple act of complimenting someone helps us seek out something positive to appreciate them even more. This works as a mental exercise for our brain to focus on the positive. Not only does the receiver feel good, but you do too. There's positivity all around! And when we seek positivity, we let go of our jealous, complaining and critical nature. A study published in *Forbes* magazine determined that being given a compliment activates the same area of the brain as when you are given a monetary reward. Moreover, being given a compliment or praise can help develop new motor skills.[41] Can you imagine?

5. Express Gratitude to Loved Ones

We have a habit of taking our loved ones for granted. We know how much they mean to us and how life would not be same without them, yet we take their presence for granted. Try to express your thankfulness to people closest to you and see how it impacts your relationship with each other. Give them a hug for taking care of you throughout the day, buy them their favourite flowers or ice cream—or simply tell them how grateful you are to have them in your life.

6. Say 'Thank You' Often

Every person we meet is battling a fight we know nothing about, and it's not possible for us to solve each problem of theirs. But there's no harm in trying! The beauty of it is that you only have to spare a few minutes of your time to thank someone for what they do. Next time a security guard opens the door for you, look him in the eye and say thank you with a smile. Thank your grocery guy or the office peon with the same smile. Offer water to your delivery man and thank him for his service. Thank people for the work they do for you. Our lives would not be the same without them. Though it has its roots in the Bhagavad Gita, Mahatma Gandhi is quoted as saying, 'Work is worship.' So when you thank someone, for their service, do it wholeheartedly.

7. Write Notes of Gratitude

I always make an effort to write a sincere thank-you note to anyone who gives me a gift, invites me to a party or thinks of me in any other way.

One more idea when writing in your journal. You can write a lengthy, heart-warming letter highlighting how grateful you are to the people and things in your life. Feel free to send it to the people you addressed it to, or simply keep it with you. You can reread it whenever you feel low, and it will help you to see the good in adverse times. As children's author Susan Lendroth says, 'To write is human, to receive a letter: Divine!'

I hope this chapter has helped you realize just how powerful gratitude can be. Whether it's expressing appreciation for the people around you, finding the silver linings in difficult situations or simply taking a moment to reflect on the good things in life, practising gratitude can make a huge difference in your happiness and overall well-being.

As someone who has personally been on the giving and receiving ends of gratitude, I can say with full confidence that it's completely worth the extra effort to make it a regular part of your life. So go ahead, jump in with both feet! You might just be surprised at how much there is to be thankful for.

4

Slow Living

⌒

Have you ever heard of slow living? It's all about ditching the hustle and bustle of modern life and taking a mindful approach. It's about connecting with your community, embracing a bigger purpose, and understanding that faster doesn't always mean better. Instead, it's about savouring each moment and finding joy in the simple things.

Let's face it, we've all been conditioned to think that if we're not constantly on the move, we're somehow failing at life. But the truth is, we're missing out on so much. It's like we're on a high-speed train that never stops—so focused on reaching the destination that we forget to enjoy the journey.

But when you slow down, you start to appreciate things in a whole new way. You notice the beauty in the world around you and find joy in the little things that you used to take for granted. It's like taking a road trip instead of flying: you never know what hidden gems you might discover along the way.

And for me, slow living has taken on a whole new meaning since I became a parent. I know it seems paradoxical given that Ashvi is two years old and always on the go. But watching my baby girl discover the ordinary things (that we take for granted) for the first time is a scintillating reminder of the awe in this world. She reminds me of the beauty and simplicity in life. Every experience is new and exciting, every new flower is a ground-breaking discovery. Every time she can stack her wooden blocks she feels like the world's greatest architect.

We've shared countless moments together—from quiet strolls through nature to lazy afternoons spent romping on the floor—which have been made even more special by embracing slow living! I really think there should be more romping in life. Maybe a room in every office building where employees can go unwind. It's been a true joy to share this phase of my life with my little one, and I can't wait to see where our slow-living journey takes us next.

It's a conscious choice, but one that can make a huge difference. As the great Thich Nhat Hanh once said, 'Smile, breathe and go slowly.' Trust me, it's worth it! So, are you ready to give it a try? Yeah, you are.

Simple Ways to Help You Slow Down

1. Do Less

Unearthing my inner logic in the pursuit of supermom/wife status, I've discovered that by tending to the essentials, I not only achieve more but also excel in every task. I know it's hard to slow down when you are trying to do a million things. Yet, make the conscious choice to do less. Focus on what's important, what needs to be done, and let the rest go.

Put space between tasks and appointments so you can move through your days at a more leisurely pace. Stop and smell the proverbial roses.

2. Be Present

It's not enough to just slow down; you need to be mindful of whatever you're doing at the time. That means when you find yourself wandering through the past or future, gently bring yourself back to the present moment. Focus on what's going on right now—your actions, your environment, the people around you. This takes practice but is essential.

> 'Life gives you plenty of time to do whatever you want to do if you stay in the present moment.'
>
> Deepak Chopra

3. Disconnect

Having my phone around is crucial, for who knows when my publisher, a doctor or even the esteemed prime minister might give me a ring? Well, perhaps not the prime minister. Nevertheless, there are occasions when I must bid adieu to technology's grip. When I embark on my writing ventures, I keep my phone on silent mode, switch off the TV and banish all intrusive notifications. It's a digital detox for the sake of creativity!

But seriously, don't always be connected to the outside world. This includes your *dearest* possession, yes, your mobile phone. Please turn it off. Put it away. Better yet, learn to leave it behind when possible. If you work on a computer or phone most of the day (like I do), have some time to disconnect so you can focus on other things, such as the world around you. Being connected all the time means you're subject to interruptions, constantly stressed about new information and at the mercy of others' demands. You don't need to be on call all the time. (Unless you're a doctor or a parent away from your child.)

4. Focus on People

This was a difficult behaviour to remedy. I had the attention span of a goldfish when I was younger. To put it better, I was not immune to distractions until I was in my twenties. That's when I came to realize I was missing out on human connection.

Too often we spend time with friends and family or meet with colleagues, but we're not really *there* with them. We talk to them but are distracted by devices; corporeally present, but not with our minds. We listen, but we're actually thinking about ourselves and what we want to say. It's a garbage heap of futility. None of us is immune to this, but with conscious effort you can shut off the outside world and be present with the people you're with. Just a little time spent with your family and friends can go a long way. It means we honestly *connect* with people rather than just meet with them.

5. Appreciate Nature

Nature is my ultimate muse, and the ocean holds a special place in my heart. Mumbai, with its urban hustle, offers a soothing respite through its inner-city sea. When in need of sandy solace, Goa becomes my go-to travel destination for its pristine beaches.

Many of us are shut up in our homes, offices and cars most of the time, and rarely do we get the chance to go outside. More often than not, even when we are outside, we're still talking on or playing with our cell phones. As an alternative, take the time to go outside and observe nature, up close and personal. Take a deep breath of fresh air and enjoy the chirping of birds and greenery. Exercise outdoors when you can, or find other outdoor activities to enjoy, such as nature walks, hiking, team games, etc. Feel the sensations of the wind and earth against your skin. Try to do this daily, by yourself or with loved ones.

'And forget not that the earth delights to feel your bare feet and the winds long to play with your hair.'

Khalil Gibran

6. Eat Slower

Instead of wolfing down your meals, eat slowly. Be mindful of each bite and delight in it. Appreciate the flavours and textures and be grateful for what you're eating. Eating slowly also has the benefits of preventing you from overeating and promoting better gut health. I suggest learning to eat more real, whole foods as well. Add some great spices (instead of fat and salt and sugar and frying for flavour) to make your taste buds dance. And on a lazy Sunday afternoon, cook your own food and savour the entire process. Just your friendly mindfulness at play.

7. Do One Task at a Time

Researchers have found that multitasking is a misnomer. In truth, you end up doing nothing properly; the human brain is just not wired that way.[42] Focus on one thing at a time. When you feel the urge to switch to other tasks, pause, breathe and pull yourself back. Slowing down and doing one thing at a time leads to more productivity, enjoyment and improved efficiency.

8. Enjoy Silence

Our lives are like a never-ending symphony of sounds: phones ringing, cars honking, TVs blaring and neighbours chattering. It's like living in the middle of a music festival, except you can never leave. But what if we took a break from the noise and indulged in some sweet, sweet silence? Imagine waking up to the gentle chirping of birds outside your window, or finding a peaceful spot in a public park where you can bask in the tranquil sounds of nature. It's like a mini-vacation from the daily grind. Sure, noise has its place, but there's something to be said for the beauty of stillness. So go ahead, take a break from the never-ending noise. Who knows, you might just find that sweet sound of silence is music to your ears.

9. Breathe

When you find yourself speeding up and stressing out, pause and take a deep breath. Then take a couple more. It may seem like a waste of time, but this is scientifically proven sound advice.[43] Really feel the air coming into your body, the air filling your lungs, and then feel the stress flowing out. By mindfully focusing on each breath, you bring yourself back to the present and slow yourself down.

So, there you have it, folks! Slow living is all about taking a step back, living intentionally and savouring the moment. It's about finding joy in the simple things and being present in the here and now. As someone who's had the privilege of learning about slow living, I can tell you first-hand that it's truly a transformative way of life. It might take a bit of practice to get used to at first, but trust me, it's worth it. So why not give it a try? You're *into* new things now! Start small and see where it takes you. Who knows, you might just find a whole new way of living that brings you more happiness and satisfaction than you ever thought possible. Live a better life. Live slowly. Sloth bears do it and they always have a smile on their faces. Seriously, don't take this seriously!

5

Minimalism

⌒

I'm sure you've come across the term 'minimalism' quite a lot in recent times. It's been all over the internet, with people recounting how they are selling all their possessions to live with just the bare essentials. But what I've discovered is that there's a lot more to this concept than just decluttering your physical space.

I have always been interested in this lifestyle. After reading books and articles on it, I found that the concept of minimalism, as pictured today, is just the Western version of something that's been part of our culture since forever—it's called aparigraha (or non-possessiveness.) The Western adaptation is fraught with more glam and possibly less depth.

What Is Aparigraha?

Aparigraha is a concept that has been around for centuries in Indian culture. It's one of the five yamas of Patanjali's Yoga Sutra (the fifth, to be precise) and one of the great vows

(Mahavrats) in Jainism. It holds much more meaning than just getting rid of material things. Minimalism is just the beginning; it's a tool to live a more meaningful life. Along with non-possessiveness, we need to practise non-attachment as well, because only then can we live a truly minimalistic life with a clutter-free mind and heart, not just a clutter-free home.

I believe we Indians have been living a minimalistic lifestyle way before it was considered 'cool'. In fact, I'm pretty sure we're the ones who *made* it cool. Mad props to us. Our traditional clothing, like sarees and dhotis, has always exuded simplicity and timeless elegance, and is crafted with natural fabrics that stand the test of time. When it comes to healing, Ayurveda and herbal remedies have been our go-to, harnessing the power of nature instead of relying on artificial concoctions. Spirituality, as I mentioned above, guides us to detach from material possessions. And let's not forget our eco-friendly practices: from rainwater harvesting to organic farming, we've always been about living in harmony with nature. So, minimalism isn't just a passing trend for us, it's a timeless philosophy that reflects our innate sense of simplicity, sustainability, and mindful living that has been part of our Indian way of life for ages.

Who is a Minimalist?

Minimalism has such a wide range of definitions. There is no right or wrong way to employ it. It's all about what works for you and *your* lifestyle. Minimalists are people who understand that to deepen our spirituality, we need to evaluate our priorities. In most major religions (including Christianity, Islam, Buddhism, Hinduism, Jainism and many others) there is some form of the practice of minimalism, which helps us to truly know ourselves.

As a spiritually inclined person, I have always felt a deep connection to something greater than myself. I have never limited myself to studying just one religion or philosophy academically. Having grown up in a Hindu family and being married to a Jain, it feels as if the universe intended for me to gather wisdom from various sources until I found what truly resonated with me.

There's so much to learn from every world and religious philosophy! I always find the time to read up on different ideologies. I adore a good book, no matter the genre. In this way, I can deepen my understanding of the divine and my place in the universe. In this pursuit, I leant on my husband. He has always been a very spiritual person, unwavering in his beliefs and in contact with many spiritual leaders. He helped me find my Guruji, who has been my guide through life and inspired me to embrace concepts such as minimalism.

In simple terms, minimalists are people who focus on what's truly essential for them. They understand the difference between their wants and needs and focus solely on the needs. Minimalism doesn't mean we *can't* own anything or that we don't care; rather, it's that we're not mentally or emotionally attached to them. We focus less on having and more on being. You can do that, right? Easy-peasy. This applies not just to our possessions, but to our goals, ideas,

Clutter = old ideas, toxic
relationships, bad habits
that are not supporting
your better self

Minimalism 147

relationships and most importantly our thought process. For a minimalist, the objective isn't to reduce: it's to eliminate distractions so they can focus on the things that are truly important.

> 'Clutter is not just physical stuff. It's old ideas, toxic relationships, and bad habits. Clutter is anything that does not support your better self.'
>
> Eleanor Brown

Perhaps you're questioning the need to return to a simpler way of life like the kind that our grandparents embraced. After all, we live in a world where we can buy almost anything with just a few clicks. But is more always better? As the saying goes, 'You can't buy happiness, but you can buy stuff to distract you from the fact that you're not happy.'

Why Consider Minimalism?

- Wealth accumulation is a potential source of greed, jealousy, and selfishness. We all know where *that* can lead us. A joint study found that people who are materialistic tend to have less ability to focus on mindfulness, and they couldn't give a hoot about sustainability.[44] Who wants to live like that?

- We were all born as minimalists, without a single thing in our hands. That means we are all capable of living that way. And when we can live lightly, why burden ourselves with petty objects?

- Think about it. Are your possessions worth the weight they add to your life? Keep a regular check on your things and their power over your mind and soul and you'll understand how they work as a manner of bondage, keeping us tied down.

- With our desire to have more, we find ourselves spending time and energy to manage and maintain everything. We try so hard that the things that were supposed to help us be happier end up ruling us instead.

- We all know that we'll end up growing tired of all the things we acquire. So what's the point of procuring something new? Why do we never get tired of this cycle? It's because we feel that having more will increase *our* worth. We're desperate to convey our significance, our value to others. We use objects to tell people just how valuable we are. I don't find much self-worth in that.

- When we stop chasing our desires, we can devote our time and energy to discovering what's genuinely meaningful in life. Will Rogers, actor and possibly America's favourite cowboy, put it best: 'Too many people spend money they haven't earned, to buy things they don't want, to impress people they don't like.'

Practical Tips to Reduce Your Possessions

In our house, we love the simplicity of weeding out possessions to include nothing more than the necessary items. It may seem like sparse living, but it really is therapeutic.

I repeat, reducing stuff is not the end game. It's the beginning. We often find it easy to do things that are tangible, something we can physically see with our own eyes. When we get in the habit of living with less in the physical world, we train our minds to live a minimalistic life mentally—and that allows us to be detached from everything unnecessary! You don't have to go be an ascetic (though that could be the ultimate goal for some of us), but start small and work your way up. Slow shifts in your lifestyle are more sustainable as opposed to sudden radical changes. Minimizing is difficult, but not impossible. Here are some helpful tips to get you going:

- Start with assigning a basket/box/bag as your 'declutter bag'. Always keep it in a reachable place. Once it is full, you can separate things according to their usage—to discard, donate, gift, etc. I have several such boxes.

- Start with the stuff you don't use or don't like. That will make it easier for you and will give you a feeling of accomplishment, pushing you to try more. Why would you keep stuff like that anyway? The things you don't use will only clutter your cabinets, and the things you don't like will put you in a bad mood every time you see them.

- The best way to get used to discarding excess things is to make it a habit. Stop hoarding in the first place. And whenever you come across something you don't use any more (and are not going to use in the near future) put it in the declutter box right away.

- Minimize anything you have in multiples. Why would you need two of the same kind of blouse? Or two radios? Get rid of one.

- The golden rule is getting rid of things you haven't used in a year.

- Discard things if they are sitting there just for the sake of appearance and not adding value to your life. You don't need that vase of artificial flowers. All they do is look fake and collect dust.

- I'm a very organized person. The habit of being organized was bred into me from a young age. But that doesn't mean I don't end up with non-essential things on occasion. Please keep this in mind: organizing is not minimizing. No matter how organized you are, if you keep *all* your things, excess is still excess. Purge!

- A place for everything and everything in its place. Have a designated place for everything you own. It will not only help you stay organized but also help you hoard less!

- There's no rule that says you need to fill all the empty storage space in the house. Embrace the idea of empty spaces. Once you get started, you'll want to have more. I find it gratifying to be able to open a closet and not have umbrellas and brooms falling on me.

- Pull up your socks now! Don't leave things till 'someday'. If you wait until you have the time, you'll never have the time.

'I don't have time is just saying it's not a priority.'

Naval Ravikant

Mental Benefits of Minimalism

1. Freedom from Attachments

I never feel sadness when I take an item out of my home. I have no attachment to it. When you realize that your possessions are just a means to live and not a part of you, you stop worrying about them, and then parting with them is not painful. You start to develop a sense of freedom. The Bhagavad Gita is very clear that attachment causes suffering. Don't suffer. Liberate yourself.

2. More Time

Time is the most precious thing you have, and when you're not constantly buying and maintaining material things, you have more time to do the things that really matter! As I stated earlier, we don't have a whole lot of things to maintain in our home, so it's easier to find the time to write, paint, worship, meditate, exercise and play with Ashvi. You too will come to find that there will be more time to focus on your hobbies, spend time with loved ones and just relax and unwind. American religious writer William Penn said, 'Time is what we want most but what we use worst.' Don't be that person.

3. Fewer Distractions

With fewer things, you'll have fewer distractions. You won't be tempted by advertisements or media, and you won't feel pressured to buy the shiny new things you absolutely do not need. This means you can focus on what's important and live a more intentional life.

4. Organized Living

I used to let Ashvi's toys stay on the floor presuming that she would inevitably take them out again the next day. Big mistake. I started feeling more tension in the house. I realized I needed to pick up her toys and put them in a basket every night or I would go loopy.

Living an organized life can make you more confident, energetic and open to new ideas. New ideas lend to your creativity, awareness, logic, intuition, problem-solving—the whole shebang. Simply put, new ideas are good for the brain. When your home and workspace are clutter-free, you can focus better and be more productive. This can lead to a sense of accomplishment and satisfaction.

5. Focus on Your Inner Self

Since I stopped having to tend to physical junk, I've had more time to do the things that matter. I even have more time to meditate and practise yoga, whatever I need most that day! There's less rushing around and more mindfulness. I really see the sky and observe passers-by going about their day.

When you stop thinking about materialistic things, you can focus more on your inner self and your higher purpose in life. You can spend more time meditating, journalling or doing other activities that help you connect with yourself and the world around you. It's a form of self-care.

6. Stop Comparing Yourself to Others

Since I cleared out all the superfluous stuff, I noticed that I didn't compare myself to other people *at all*. I mean, I didn't do a whole lot of that, to begin with, but the effects were felt all the same.

When you practice minimalism, you stop comparing yourself to others. You realize that you don't need to have the latest gadgets or the trendiest clothes to be happy. This lifestyle can help you gain more confidence in yourself and be more content with your life.

> 'Comparison is the most poisonous element in the human heart because it destroys ingenuity, and it robs peace and joy.'
>
> Euginia Herlihy

7. Worry Less about Other People's Judgement

I believe with my whole heart that what people think of me is more a reflection of them than me. Besides, it isn't any of my business to know what they think of me. That's their problem. When you accept a certain way of living for yourself, you stop worrying about what other people think of you. Who cares what they think anyway? It's *your* opinion that matters. When you're not concerned about impressing others with your possessions or lifestyle, you can focus on being true to yourself.

8. More Financial Freedom

When you have fewer possessions, your minimum living costs decrease, which means you'll have more freedom to choose your job or pursue your passions. This can give you a sense of financial security and independence. Financial security is gold—and if you can reach it doing what you love, it's like cherry on the cake.

Remember, minimalism is not just a trend or a catchphrase; it's a way of life that can bring us a sense of freedom, clarity and purpose. Whether you choose to adopt a minimalist lifestyle or not, the principles of non-possessiveness and non-attachment can be valuable reminders of what really matters. So take a moment to reflect on what brings you joy and meaning, and let that guide your choices and actions. Remember, less is often more when it comes to living a happy, fulfilling life.

6

Conscious Consumption

~

In adulthood, it's tough to limit ourselves to buying what we need. If I am won over by an advertisements, and later figure out that I don't actually need or want that product, then what should I do?

We're constantly bombarded with messages about what we should buy, how much we should buy, and what we need to be happy. The truth is, consuming mindlessly can leave us feeling empty and unfulfilled. That's why we should make a conscious effort to practise mindful consumption. You meditate, you're mindful, you practice minimalism— you're already happy, aren't you? Now we're adding mindful consumption to amplify that mood. How about *that*?

And as a part of society, I believe it is our moral responsibility to live sustainably. We only have one Earth, and our current actions are causing irreparable damage to it. Sustainability simply means minimizing our negative impact on the world and the planet. It may sound challenging at first, but it is surprisingly easy to do.

The Four 'R's of Sustainability

Reduce, reuse, recycle, repair—sounds poetic, but how can we implement these principles in our lives? Lately, we see most new brands labelling themselves as 'sustainable brands', but when we check the prices of their products, they are far from sustainable for our budget. You may have all that extra cash floating around because of your newfound minimalism, but why pay unnecessarily? We think we can never afford a sustainable life, but let me tell you a secret. When you start thinking in the right direction and taking small steps towards a sustainable lifestyle, you will realize that you don't *need* those fancy brands. In fact, your cost of living will reduce drastically.

Easy Ways to Live a Sustainable Life

1. Avoid Fast Fashion

It's hard *not* to want to be on trend all the time, I get it. The people in ads are flashing their perfect smiles wearing the hottest clothes. They're having fun and being popular, and it's *clearly* because of the clothes, right?

I decided to go three whole months without buying a stitch of clothing, no matter the occasion, no matter the discount. I waded through my closet and created an outfit from material I already had. I learnt to mix and match—a hem here, a stitch there, take this up, loosen this buckle, and voilà! I had a whole new wardrobe without spending a single rupee!

Knowing that I could put together a complete outfit from my own closet has promoted my self-confidence and drive. I no longer waste time shopping from the sales racks or waiting for a holiday sale. I can focus on what really matters, like reading or Ashvi. I feel better about myself, knowing that I'm another step away from being part of a global problem.

One of the best things we can do for ourselves is to stop running behind fast fashion. Instead, focus on quality fabrics that suit the climate and go for timeless styles. When your outfits have a simple style and colour, they will be easy to use in multiple ways, mixing and matching. Don't fall prey to trends and fads; they are an enormous waste of money and resources, and they only last for one season. Did you know that there are over 1 million tonnes of textile waste generated every year in India?[45] The United States throws out over *eleven times* that figure.

> 'Don't be into trends. Don't make fashion own you, but you decide what you are.'
>
> Gianni Versace

2. Say No to Single-Use Products

Initially, I thought it would be extremely difficult to change my lifestyle. It turned out to be effortless. It's a rewarding feat to say, 'Absolutely not!' to single-use products. Even if they are biodegradable, they are still a waste of resources. Make it a rule to not use anything which can't be reused. You just have to make a firm decision, and you'll be successful.

3. Pay Attention to Packaging

Whenever you buy an item, pay attention to the packaging along with the product. See if there's any way to minimize the packaging or perhaps find packaging sturdy enough to be reused.

4. Stop Using Plastic

Plastic is one of the biggest threats to our planet, and we need to stop using it as much as possible. I was horrified when I read a study about microplastics being found in the human placenta.[46] Though I haven't been able to cut it out completely, I make conscious efforts to minimize its use. Many brands are now conscientiously trying to take steps towards sustainability, and you can find loads of eco-friendly alternatives within your budget. For example, one of the least taxing things you can do is bring your own reusable bags when you go grocery shopping.

5. Opt for Repair Instead of Purchase

Let's get back to the age-old art of repairing things instead of buying new products. We all are guilty of throwing away a good item because it had a minor problem. We *do* think about the money we're going to spend, but we forget to consider all the resources that went into making it. Let's try to repair what can be repaired. And this art will help you not just with your things, but also your relationships with people. Try it once. Or twice. Maybe three times or more. You will feel a sense of great accomplishment.

6. Buy Local

A simple way to reduce your carbon footprint is by buying your everyday essentials from local stores. This not only supports small businesses in your community, but also saves the packaging needed to wrap and deliver your products, and the transportation charges! According to researchers at Michigan State University, buying locally means that fewer materials are used in packaging, therefore there's reduced strain on landfills, and consequently less traffic on roads.[47]

'Conserving energy and thus saving money, reducing consumption of unnecessary products and packaging and shifting to a clean-energy economy would likely hurt the bottom line of polluting industries, but would undoubtedly have positive effects for most of us.'

David Suzuki

The Golden Rules of Living Mindfully

For me, doing the right thing has become as easy as breathing. When I do falter, I feel a sudden urge to quickly find my moral compass, because my daughter deserves to live in a world that's nothing less than awesome. I've inherited this unwavering moral compass from my father (by now you all know he is my hero!), who taught me to always do the right thing, even when nobody's watching. He instilled in me the values of taking responsibility for my surroundings, speaking the truth even when it's hard, and not seeking approval or recognition for doing the right thing. So yeah, I'm all about doing the right thing, and I'll keep doing it, whether anyone notices or not.

There are some simple but important rules we should all follow.

1. Don't Do to Others What You Don't Want Done to Yourself

I was raised by this rule and that's exactly how I'm raising Ashvi. She's only a toddler, but I think she's getting the hang of it. The golden rule of 'Treat others the way you want to be treated' is found in many religions. This fundamental principle applies not just to humans, but to all living beings. It reminds us to treat others with the kindness, respect and compassion with which we would like to be treated ourselves. This behaviour isn't limited to humans, as it so happens: animals, plants and all living beings deserve this basic courtesy. I treat my plants with so much kindness and respect that I think they're becoming spoilt.

When we consume mindfully, we not only take care of ourselves but also the world we live in. And then we can cultivate a more harmonious and compassionate world, where all beings can thrive and flourish. Simple as that!

2. Don't Take Anything if You Don't Have the Right

I never thought about this before. When I meditated, of course I would give thanks for the house I lived in, my family, my friends, but I never thought about thanking the universe for the basic resources I had. It goes even deeper. Have you ever stopped to think about the things you take for granted every day? The water you use to take a shower, the vegetables you get, the clothes you wear—these are all resources we need to survive. Have you ever thought about the impact that your consumption of these resources has on the environment and other people?

As a society, we tend to take resources for granted without considering the impact our consumption has on others. We think that just because we can afford to buy something, we have the right to use it. But this is neither true nor rational. We need to understand that we do not have a boundless right to consume resources.

It's vital we remember that resources are finite and need to be shared. We need to be mindful of our consumption and ensure that we are not taking more than our fair share. Think of the penguins and quokkas! (Quokkas rival sloths when it comes to being the happiest animals on the planet. That's not scientific or anything, but they're always smiling and cute as heck!)

3. Understand the Facets of Fearlessness

Being fearless is often seen as a positive trait. We admire those who have the courage to take risks and face challenges head on. We all probably wanted to be intrepid superheroes at some point. However, it's important to remember that fearlessness is only a good thing when it's used for the right reasons.

There are many things in life that we *should* be afraid of, such as causing harm to others or the environment. The fear of doing wrong should never go away. If we lose this fear, we risk causing irreparable damage to ourselves and the world around us. We should always have a healthy fear of the consequences of our actions and use this feeling to guide us towards doing the right thing.

'Doing the right thing isn't always easy—in fact, sometimes it's real hard; but just remember that doing the right thing is always right.'

David Cottrell

My Journey

As I embarked on my journey towards mindful consumption, I was forced to confront my own wasteful habits and the environmental impact of my actions. But instead of feeling defeated, I embraced the challenge with open arms. It was a journey of self-discovery and growth, a chance to redefine who I was and what I stood for.

At first, it was difficult to break away from the allure of mindless consumerism and make more conscious choices. But as I learnt more about sustainability and its impact on the world, I began to see the bigger picture. I started to buy reusable products and clothes made from sustainable materials and shopped for food locally to reduce my carbon footprint. It wasn't always easy, but the rewards were undeniable.

By consuming mindfully, I found that I was more content and fulfilled with the things I already had. I no longer felt the need to constantly seek out new items to make me happy, as

I had discovered the joy in appreciating what I already had. And as a bonus, I was spending less money on unnecessary items and making a positive impact on the environment. As Marianne Williamson once said, 'Every decision you make reflects your evaluation of who you are.'

And through mindful consumption, I have become more intentional and thoughtful about the choices I make. It's a small but powerful way to live out my values and leave a positive impact on the world, for my daughter and future generations.

Remember This!

At the core of mindful consumption is the idea of being intentional and thoughtful about our choices. It's about recognizing that our actions have a profound impact on the world around us and taking responsibility for that impact. It's about being aware of the resources we use and the waste we produce, and making choices that align with our values and beliefs.

I want to emphasize that sustainable living is not an all-or-nothing approach. We don't need to be perfect, and we don't need to make dramatic changes overnight. We need to take small, intentional steps towards a more sustainable lifestyle and be mindful of our impact on the environment. This environment is the one we were given. It's our duty to take care of her. Every small action can make a difference, and together we can work towards a more sustainable future.

Self-Study

Exercises

1. Take a mindful walk, paying attention to the sights, sounds and sensations around you.
2. During daily tasks such as brushing your teeth or washing dishes, focus on the present moment and the sensations in your body.
3. Use a timer to break up your work into manageable chunks of time.
4. Make a gratitude jar. Whenever something makes you happy, write it down on a piece of paper and put the note in the jar. Keep the jar in a place where you can see it all the time.
5. Set aside time to do something that brings you joy, such as reading or spending time in nature.
6. Take a break from social media and technology for a certain period of time every day.
7. Declutter one area of your home or workspace.

Journalling Prompts

- What were some challenges you faced while trying to stay present during daily tasks?
- How did you feel when you were able to prioritize and complete your most important tasks?

- Write down three things you are grateful for every morning.
- What activities brought you the most joy during the week?
- What did you notice about your thoughts and emotions when you slowed down and focused on being present in the moment?
- What changes did you notice in your daily routine when you simplified your decision-making process?

PART 4
THE PILLARS OF GOODNESS

1

The Power of Kindness

Have you ever experienced the uplifting feeling that comes with a simple act of kindness? Maybe it was a smile from a stranger, a thoughtful note from a friend or a generous gesture from a colleague. Whatever it was, it likely made your day a little brighter and filled your heart with warmth. It made you smile and be-bop around all day. Don't be afraid to admit it.

Kindness is the simple act of showing concern, consideration and generosity towards others without expecting anything in return. When we are kind to others, we create a ripple effect that spreads far beyond our immediate surroundings. It can inspire others to be kind, creating a positive feedback loop that can change the world. It's like the butterfly effect. This theory states that if a butterfly flaps its wings in Ecuador, it can cause a tsunami in India through a seemingly unrelated chain of events.

'To be kind is good. To be kind without expecting anything in return is better.'

Tariq Ramadan

Why Is Kindness So Important?

The answer lies in the science of human connection. We are social creatures who thrive on connection, and kindness is one of the most powerful ways to foster this connection. It's one of the reasons *Homo sapiens* survived; we were and are social beings. When we are kind to others, we create a sense of belonging and community that can lead to greater feelings of happiness and fulfilment. A study was done on the effects of community, and it was found that those who were involved with their communities were healthier than those with poor community connections.[48]

Keep in mind that the benefits of kindness aren't limited to the recipient. When we are kind to others, we also experience a sense of satisfaction and fulfilment. Like when we pay someone a compliment, we feel good about ourselves and our actions, which can boost our self-esteem and confidence.

'Kindness is the sunshine in which virtue grows.'

Robert Green Ingersoll

A Mayo Clinic study found that people who practise kindness regularly experience a range of health benefits, including reduced stress, increased happiness, improved relationships and better physical health—that means lower blood pressure and lower cortisol levels. Being kind to others can lead to a longer life span, in essence.

1. Fill Yourself with Utmost Love and Kindness

I'm not always as successful at this as I'd like, but showing myself compassion is a new trick up my sleeve. As my grandfather always says, 'We can only give what we possess.' So, if we want to be kind to others, we must begin by filling ourselves with utmost love and kindness. This means being gentle with ourselves by forgiving our mistakes and treating ourselves with the same compassion we would show to a dear friend. We deserve it!

When we fill ourselves with love and kindness, we become a source of positive energy for those around us. We radiate joy and warmth, and others are naturally drawn to us. This can create a positive feedback loop where our kindness inspires others to be kind, and their kindness inspires us to be even kinder.

2. Live While Being Open-Minded, Open-Hearted and Open-Handed

To be truly kind, we must live open-minded, open-hearted and open-handed lives. Living in this way can be challenging, especially if we are used to approaching the world with a closed mind and heart. However, it's important to remember that kindness is not about being perfect or having all the answers. It's about being willing to try, to learn, and to grow.

'Man's mind, once stretched by a new idea, never regains its original dimensions.'

Oliver Wendell Holmes

Living with an open mind means being curious and willing to learn from others, even if their perspectives differ from our own. Living open-heartedly means cultivating empathy and compassion for others, seeing the world through their eyes and being kind even when it's not easy. But we're kindness warriors at this point. We can overcome *anything*! Living open-handedly means being generous with our time, resources and talents, and being willing to give without expecting anything in return. As motivational speaker Brian Tracy says, 'Always give without remembering and always receive without forgetting.'

3. Focus on What is True, Good and Useful

In our fast-paced world, it can be easy to get caught up in negative or harmful thoughts and behaviours. We may find ourselves consumed with worries and anxieties or in gossip and drama. However, this kind of negativity can be toxic to our mental and emotional well-being. It's a poisonous pickle.

To combat this, it's important to focus on what is good, true and useful. This means letting go of negative thoughts and behaviours, and instead focusing on things that uplift us and others. Studies show that when people are enthusiastic and optimistic in life, it positively affects their psychological and physical health—but they're also able to handle it better when things go sideways.[49] We can cultivate this by reading positive news stories, practising gratitude and focusing on positive affirmations. We can also seek out inspiring role models who embody kindness and compassion and strive to emulate their behaviour in our own lives.

4. Let Go of Ego

Ego. We all have one. Mine is pretty well in check, but I still have moments of envy because I'm human. One of the greatest barriers to kindness is a sense of self-importance. When we think we are the most important person in the world, we become self-centred and unable to see the needs of others. We may even become resentful or jealous when others receive attention or praise. I've never really had delusions of grandeur or anything, but I've been self-centred on occasion, especially when I was in my teens. According to German author and scholar Eckhart Tolle, the ego is the voice in your head. It's excited when you confirm that someone is wrong, and it enjoys judging people. It's everything we're trying not to be!

To be kind, we must let go of our ego and focus on others. We must recognize that we are all interconnected and that our happiness is inextricably linked to the happiness of those around us. When we let go of our ego and focus on the needs of others, we tap into a source of positive energy that can bring us closer to our own happiness.

'When the ego dies, the soul awakes.'

Mahatma Gandhi

5. Don't Give Up on Humanity

Watching the news can be dispiriting. My husband and I have an agreement that we can watch or read the news, but it stops there. We can *discuss* current events, but we cannot become emotionally invested in what's happening. It's somehow natural for us to focus on the negative, and I don't want that toxic waste in my house.

It's easy to feel discouraged by the negativity and conflict we see in the world around us. We may feel overwhelmed by the magnitude of the problems, unsure of how we can make a difference. However, it's important to remember that no matter how bad things may seem, there is always hope. When we give up on humanity, we give up on ourselves. We lose sight of the power of kindness and the positive impact we can have on others. Instead, we must cultivate a sense of optimism and faith in our ability to create change. We must believe that even small acts of kindness can make a difference and that every person has the capacity to create positive change in the world. A study at Harvard University showed that optimism makes you cool as a cucumber in situations of high stress, and also increases your lifespan.[50] This is like the fourth piece of advice that can increase your lifespan. At this rate, you're going to be immortal!

6. Small Acts of Kindness

Sometimes it's as simple as making my husband a mild cup of coffee with a drop of milk and sugar in the morning or telling a stranger that I love their outfit. At other times, it's more like painting a graffitied wall in the middle of the night under the cover of darkness. It's the kind of things that make someone memorable. Be that memory!

It's important to take note that not all kind gestures or actions we take will be easy; many of them will go unnoticed. But that doesn't mean they aren't worth doing. Every act of kindness, no matter how small, has the power to make a difference in someone's life. It's like dropping a pebble into a pond: the ripples may be small, but they can spread far and wide. This action is appropriately named 'the ripple effect'.

And even if the world doesn't see our acts of kindness, that doesn't mean they go unnoticed. The universe has a way of balancing things out, and our good deeds will always come back to us, even if we don't see it at the time. If you see stray litter blowing across the street, pick it up and throw it away.

'Carry out a random act of kindness, with no expectation of reward, safe in the knowledge that one day someone might do the same for you.'

Princess Diana

Simple Ways to Practise Kindness Every Day

- A smile can brighten someone's day and make them feel seen and valued.

- A thoughtful note or text message can lift someone's spirits and remind them that they are not alone. You text all day long. Put it to good use.
- Offering to help someone with a task, no matter how small, can make them feel supported and cared for.
- Donating to a charity or volunteering for a cause can make a real difference. It makes you feel all gooey inside too, so it's a two-fer.
- Holding the door open for someone, giving up your seat on the bus or train, or letting someone go ahead of you in a queue can make a big difference to someone's day. I often let people go ahead of me in a queue if they have fewer items than me, and I always hold the door open for someone if we get to the door at the same time.
- Listening to someone with empathy and judgement can help them feel heard and understood.

In a world that can often feel cold and uncaring, kindness is a beacon of light. It has the power to break down barriers and bring people together, regardless of their differences. As reported by a group of neuroscientists from Stanford University, showing a little kindness can increase your levels of oxytocin and dopamine (the love and happiness chemicals in the brain). It can also reduce stress and improve your physical and mental health.[51] It's a reminder that we're all human, and we all have struggles and challenges to overcome. When we show kindness to others, we create a sense of unity and compassion that can transform the world.

Kindness is a practice, and it takes time and effort to cultivate. But the rewards are immeasurable for us and those around us. So let's try to make kindness a habit, not unlike blinking or breathing. Look for opportunities to show kindness to others every day, no matter how small it may seem. And watch as that kindness spreads, fabricating a kind of contagious positivity that touches countless lives. Together, let's create a world that values kindness above all else.

'No act of kindness, no matter how small,
is ever wasted.'

Aesop

2

The Art of Empathy and Compassion

Have you ever felt like you just can't seem to connect with others or develop a deep bond? It's a struggle that many of us face, but the key to overcoming it may be simpler than you think. The answer lies in cultivating empathy and compassion. And a little compassion stretches on and on. These two qualities are often overlooked, but they have the power to transform your relationships and even make a positive impact on the world around you. So, let's dive in and explore how we can develop these qualities and unlock a happier, more fulfilling life.

What's the Difference?

Empathy and compassion are often used interchangeably, but there is a significant difference between the two. Empathy is the ability to understand and share the feelings of others, while compassion is the desire to alleviate their suffering.

As the Dalai Lama XIV said, 'Compassion is the wish to see others free from suffering.' You understand. Together, they form a powerful combination that can improve our relationships and promote happiness and well-being.

When we practise empathy and compassion, we are more likely to connect with others on a deeper level. We can understand their perspective, validate their feelings and offer support when needed. We know how to look at other perspectives. This not only strengthens our relationships but also creates a sense of community and belonging.

Empathy and compassion can also help reduce conflicts and improve communication. When we take the time to understand someone's point of view and show compassion for their struggles, we are more likely to find common ground and resolve conflicts in a peaceful manner.

'Empathy is seeing with the eyes of another, listening with the ears of another, and feeling with the heart of another.'

Alfred Adler

My Story

When I had Ashvi, I was completely overwhelmed. As much as I loved her, I found myself struggling to adjust to the demands of parenthood. I was sleep-deprived, anxious and felt like I had no idea what I was doing. That's when one of my closest friends stepped in. We'll call her Vedika.

One day, Vedika showed up at my doorstep with a bag of groceries and a smile. She told me she was there to help in any way she could. She took my baby for a walk, while I took a much-needed nap, and she even helped with my chores. But it wasn't just the practical help that made a difference. It was the way she listened to me and showed genuine empathy for what I was going through.

Vedika is a mother herself, so she understood the challenges and turbulent range of emotions that come with being one. She never judged me or made me feel like I was failing. Instead, she gave me a listening ear and words of encouragement. Though she hadn't gone through postpartum depression herself, she could imagine the depths of its darkness. Her compassion and empathy made me feel seen and supported during one of the most vulnerable times in my life. Thanks to her kindness and understanding, I was able to navigate the challenges of new motherhood with more ease and confidence.

Through this experience, I learnt first-hand how powerful empathy and compassion can be. They can throw us a life raft when we feel like we're drowning, and they remind us that we're not alone in our struggles. So, if you're going through a difficult time or know someone who is, remember the power of empathy and compassion. It can make all the difference in the world. It may not be easy, but it will be invaluable.

Practical Ways to Cultivate Empathy and Compassion

1. Listen Actively

When Vedika was helping me through my postpartum phase, the greatest thing she did for me was listen to me earnestly. Other friends and family members (who visited unannounced) 'listened' to give me advice. She really heard me.

One of the most important aspects of empathy is actively listening to others. This means giving your full attention to the person speaking, asking questions and showing that you care about their perspective. By doing this, you'll be able to understand their feelings and experiences on a deeper level.

2. Offer Help

If you see someone in need, offer to help in any way that you can. This could be as simple as holding the elevator door open for someone who didn't quite make it or offering a listening ear. It's important to follow through on these offers, and not just use them to feel better about yourself.

'Actions speak louder than words.'

St Anthony of Padua

Try to imagine yourself in the other person's position. How would you feel if you were going through the same situation? What would you want someone to say or do for you? By putting yourself in their shoes, you can more clearly understand their perspective and respond with newfound empathy and compassion.

3. Show Kindness to Strangers

Something special happens when a stranger shows me courtesy. I glow. Then, I pay the gesture forward to someone else who will hopefully continue the trend. Smile at someone who looks like they might be having a bad day, hold the door open for someone or offer a kind word to a stranger. This behaviour can go a long way. A study at the University of Chicago revealed that random acts of kindness can have an enormous effect on the giver and the recipient.[52] The giver walks away feeling lighter and cheerier while the recipient shimmers for the rest of the day.

Self-Compassion

After months of postpartum depression, I decided that I'd experienced more than my fair share of darkness in what should be the most joyous moments of life. So, while I was feeling the weight on my heart, I decided to fumble my way through a little thing called self-compassion. I finally recognized that I couldn't be compassionate or empathetic towards others if I wasn't cultivating these qualities towards myself.

Compassion begins with yourself. Be kind and forgiving to yourself and treat yourself with the same care and understanding that you would offer to others. This means not beating yourself up over mistakes, recognizing your own needs and emotions and taking care of yourself mentally and physically. By doing so, you'll be better equipped to show empathy and compassion towards others.

With a *lot* of work, I slogged my way off that wretched path of postpartum depression, and I finally feel like myself again.

In conclusion, empathy and compassion are not just important for the well-being of others, but also for our own personal growth and happiness. By understanding and sharing in the experiences of those around us, we can connect on a deeper level and feel less alone in our struggles. And by focusing on the needs and feelings of others, we can experience a sense of purpose and fulfilment that can lead to greater satisfaction and happiness in life.

So, let's make a conscious effort to be more empathetic and compassionate towards those in our lives, and watch as our own happiness and well-being flourish as a result.

3

Giving Back

As part of my ascent out of postpartum depression, I had a significant realization: I had become somewhat self-centred. My thoughts had revolved solely around myself for a while, which contradicted the values instilled in me by my parents. It was crucial for me to shift my focus and begin considering the well-being of others. With determination, I embarked on a transformative path.

As human beings, we are hardwired to crave happiness and contentment. We look for ways to achieve this through different means, such as pursuing our passions, building connections or achieving success in our careers. However, one of the most fulfilling ways to achieve happiness is by giving back to society and nature.

Now, you may say that people have been cruel to you, or they don't treat you well—so why give them anything but matching deeds? Remember, when you do something for others, it is not about giving to other people, but about giving to the greater good, to the world we live in, and to the environment that sustains us. It allows us to connect with the world around us, make a positive impact, and experience a sense of inner peace and fulfilment. (Remember this song Michael Jackson sang in the early 90s? 'Heal the world, make it a better place, for you and for me and the entire human race.'

The Benefits of Giving Back

- *Increased Happiness and Well-Being:* When we give back, we experience a sense of satisfaction and fulfilment that can't be found in any other way. I can personally substantiate this claim. I'm sure you could too.

- *Improved Mental Health:* Giving back not only benefits others but also boosts our own mental health. Volunteering has been scientifically proven to diminish the grip of depression and anxiety, while enhancing our psychological well-being. So why not lend a helping hand and discover that the best prescription for a healthy mind might just be a generous dose of kindness?

- *Stronger Communities:* I recall when our neighbourhood was hit by a devastating flood, in 2006. In that challenging time, when the water rose, we united as a community, offering shelter, supplies, and support to those affected. It was in those moments of collective effort and care that I witnessed the true power of unity, turning neighbours into friends and transforming the community into a vibrant tapestry of support. By extending a helping hand, we not only uplift others but also find our own place in the beautiful patchwork of humanity.

- *Positive Impact on the Environment:* By volunteering with environmental organizations or making environmentally conscious choices in our daily lives, we can reduce our impact on the planet and create a more sustainable future. Less carbon footprint, healthier earth. Don't leave your metaphorical footprint anywhere.

Ways to Give Back

There is a vast abundance of opportunities to give back to society and the world at large! Now that we understand the importance and benefits of giving back, let's explore some practical ways to do so.

1. Volunteer Your Time

Whenever possible, I like to help children in need. It's a gratifying experience to give a piece of yourself to another human being, a mark of respect for those you help. One of the easiest and most effective ways to give back is to volunteer your time. Give time to your local community kitchen, work with women and children in need, help plant a community garden or pack boxes of medical supplies for distribution to health camps. There are innumerable opportunities to get involved and make a positive impact.

A group study has shown that as a result of volunteering, we experience what's called the 'helper's high': that warm feeling you get when you do something good for others.[53]

2. Donate to a Worthy Cause

If you're not able to volunteer your time, consider donating to a worthy cause instead. Whether a charity, non-profit organization or community, there are myriad organizations that rely on donations to carry out their important work.

3. Be Kind and Generous

Finally, remember that giving back isn't just about formal volunteering or donations. Small acts of kindness and generosity can also make a significant difference in the lives of those around us. Whether it's helping a neighbour with groceries, complimenting a stranger or simply being there for a friend in need, every act of kindness and generosity counts.

'Every minute of every hour of every day you are making the world just as you are making yourself, and you might as well do it with generosity and kindness and style.'

Rebecca Solnit

Principles of Giving Back

1. Patience

As a first-time mum, I found that I needed a veritable ocean of patience. Nothing like a screaming infant at four o'clock in the morning to teach you a lesson. It's like a crash course in the art of patience, served with a side of sleep deprivation. Remember those agonizing moments of waiting for exam scores? Well, honing the fine skills of mindfulness and patience during those seemingly eternal intervals is the ultimate test of endurance.

Patience is a virtue that is often overlooked in today's fast-paced world, but it's essential when it comes to giving back. Remember that time when there was a screaming toddler with her mum in front of you while you waited in the queue? Patience. Change takes time, and it's important to be patient and persistent in our efforts to make a difference. Your patience will be both appreciated and rewarded as even small actions can add up to significant change over time.

2. Honesty

'Honesty is the best policy'; well, not exactly. It's better described as a principle that we should respect and uphold in all aspects of our lives. When it comes to giving back, it's important to be honest with ourselves and others about our actions and intentions. We should strive to act with integrity and transparency and be accountable for our words and deeds. A recent study indicated that the happier we are, the likelier we are to display complete honesty—so keep working on all the tips suggested thus far![54] Our words and deeds are the finest way to show the world our integrity.

3. Acting

We can't change anything or make progress by just sitting back and thinking about it. We need to act upon our words. Giving back requires action, whether it's volunteering our time, donating money or advocating for change. Agreeing to help your friend move out of their apartment means nothing if there is no follow-through. We must be willing to take the first step and make a commitment to making a difference.

4. Empowerment

Ashish and I try to be our bright and bold selves with Ashvi as much as possible. It's crucial for a child to grow in an environment that fosters a positive self-image and strong self-confidence, coated in a cheery disposition for a little crunchy flavour! It enables them to become hale and hearty children and adults, with healthy bodies, minds, and souls. We must empower those who need it. It is our duty as fellow citizens of this planet.

If you want to empower others, you first need to start living the most empowered version of yourself. This means taking care of your physical, mental and emotional well-being, so you can be a constructive influence in the world. When we are happy and fulfilled, we are more likely to inspire and empower others to do the same. We need to be a positive force, not only for our children and families but also for the whole world to emulate.

5. Purposeful Giving

Only a person with the right conduct, character and integrity can inspire. When we act with integrity and lead by example, we inspire others to do the same. Giving back is not just about doing good deeds; it's about embodying the values and principles that we want to see in the world. Cultural anthropologist and author Margaret Mead advised,

'Never doubt that a small group of thoughtful, committed, citizens can change the world. Indeed, it is the only thing that ever has.'

We have an innate desire for happiness and contentment. However, these feelings can be fleeting if we only focus on ourselves. To live a happy and rewarding life, it is important to learn the joys of giving instead of always receiving. Don't be selfish, be benevolent! It feels better, like a warm blanket. Giving back helps us break free from consumerism and self-centredness and allows us to connect with the world in a meaningful way. It also helps us value relationships, community and shared experiences.

Above all else, let us remember the paramount truth: Through selfless giving, we not only uplift others but also nurture a profound sense of fulfilment and purpose within ourselves, surpassing the value of any material possession.

Self-Study

Exercises

1. Write a thank-you note. Think of someone who has made a positive impact on your life and write them a heartfelt thank-you note. It could be a friend, family member or even a stranger who has shown you kindness.
2. Give a compliment. Try to give at least one sincere compliment to someone each day this week.
3. Volunteer. Find a local charity or organization that resonates with you and volunteer your time this week. It costs nothing, and you'll feel renewed.

Journalling Prompts

- How have you experienced kindness? How did it make you feel?
- What are some barriers that prevent you from being kind? How can you overcome them?
- How do you typically respond when someone shares their feelings with you? Do you tend to offer advice or simply listen?
- What are some ways you can practise empathy in your daily life?
- How do you feel when someone shows you empathy? How can you extend that same kindness to others?
- What does giving back mean to you?

PART 5

BUILDING POSITIVE RELATIONSHIPS

1

How to Love and be Loved

A shish, my parents, my in-laws and I lavish Ashvi with so much love every day to make sure she feels confident in her place in our home. The love then spreads amongst our entire household, from person to person. We have our disagreements, sure (which family doesn't?) but we never speak to each other with anything but respect. We are happier, healthier, more self-assured people because of the love that permeates our home. But we're DEFINITELY not perfect. I just want to make that clear.

Love is such a huge part of our lives, but sometimes it feels like we need a degree to understand it! But in all honesty, it's not that complicated. There are no hard and fast rules to love: all you need is a good heart and great intentions.

So, how do we give and receive love in a way that really counts? The kind of love that lasts a lifetime? It might seem simple, but it can be relatively challenging to put into practice. Let's start with breaking down some common myths about love.

Myth #1

You need to constantly shower your partner with love and adoration.

Let's face it, no one can be perfect all the time, including your partner (though they might have seemed to be when you first got together). You're both unique individuals with different likes, dislikes and moods. It's unrealistic to expect yourself or your partner to always be head over heels in love. You can still care for and respect someone without being totally infatuated with them 24/7. You still need to sleep, eat and shower. Just like you practise looking at and understanding yourself, you can recognize and accept your partner's flaws.

Myth #2

Your partner is responsible for your happiness.

Movies have done a great job of romanticizing the idea that we're only complete when we have a significant other. Who doesn't love a good rom-com? But the truth is, your happiness is your own responsibility. It's essential to love and value yourself first, so you can bring your best self to the relationship. Yes, it's lovely to have someone to share experiences with, but your partner shouldn't be the only source of your happiness.

'Happiness is an inside job. Don't assign anyone else that much power over your life.'

Mandy Hale

Myth #3

Your partner will change to fit your desires.

Let's be real, people *can* change, but only if they want to. Don't go into a relationship expecting your partner to change for you. It's not going to happen, and it shouldn't happen. You wouldn't want to change yourself for them, would you? If someone tells you they're not ready for a committed relationship, believe them and move on. If you're looking for a long-term relationship, that's a red flag any way you slice it. Don't waste your time trying to change someone into your ideal partner. Respect people when they tell you who they are and decide whether to accept them or walk away. Now go, find your ideal partner.

Don't worry if you're single and feeling like this chapter isn't for you. You can still celebrate the love that's already around you! When you appreciate the love you already have, you'll attract *more* love and happiness. You can be grateful for the love of your family and best friends or even an act of kindness from a stranger. In fact, *be* that stranger doling out kindness. It's a great feeling! Take a moment to thank the universe for the gift of life and unconditional love. Love is all around us if we only open our eyes to it.

'To be brave is to love someone unconditionally, without expecting anything in return.'

Madonna Ciccone

Tools to Help You Maintain Relationships

- Relationships work best only when we all have low expectations from others and high expectations from ourselves. We should focus on how we can help others instead of expecting them to do everything for us. Start small. Scale up from there. Psychologist Barry Schwartz says, 'The secret to happiness is having low expectations.'

- It's not your words but your actions that matter. So, if you really mean something, show it through your actions. This is the time for you to stop yapping and start moving—on your words, that is.

- People are always more important than things, but sometimes we forget this. It's important to be mindful and put people first.

- Relationships are like plants; they need constant care to survive. Work hard on your relationships every day, just like you would water a plant. There are no shortcuts in love.

- Support the one you love in all possible ways. That also means guiding them when they are on the wrong path. A little guidance goes a looooong way.

- Love and selfishness can't coexist. If you want to maintain a healthy relationship, you need to let go of your selfishness. Self-care is always allowed, but selfishness is a no-go. In Erich Fromm's words, 'Selfish persons are incapable of loving others, but they are not capable of loving themselves either.'

- Being attentive in all your relationships is crucial. Don't take people for granted, and always be grateful for the love and support they give you. They won't be there forever, so appreciate them today.

- To maintain a lifelong relationship with someone, you need to learn to let go of small issues and focus on the bigger picture. It's all about mutual understanding and compromise.

So, it's up to you to take responsibility for the state of every relationship you have. If you want to bring about real change, you need to give it your all and then some. Love yourself deeply, show others love without expecting anything in return, speak their love language, and appreciate all the love that surrounds you. When you do this, happiness will follow closely behind.

'Love has nothing to do with what you are expecting to get—only with what you are expecting to give—which is everything.'

Katharine Hepburn

Receiving Love

When I first crossed paths with Ashish, I was ready for a relationship (well, maybe not exactly). Our connection unfolded through the magical realm of books. As I embarked on writing my debut book, Ashish, having just completed a captivating novella, generously offered his assistance in navigating the perplexing challenges that arose. Eagerly, I accepted his help, and before I knew it, my book was published. Our collaboration expanded into the realm of content creation, where Ashish showcased his expertise. Over the years, our bond grew stronger.

However, when we officially began dating, Ashish displayed an astonishingly sweet demeanour, bringing me flowers and penning heartfelt poems. It was truly unbelievable! And naturally, the question lurking in my mind was, 'Why?' Now, I won't pretend that I was raised to be suspicious of every person I encountered, but considering the early stage of our relationship, I couldn't help but be perplexed by his abundant affection. It took some time, but eventually, I let my guard down and embraced the fact that he was genuine.

You see, I understand the intricacies and hesitations that come with accepting and receiving love. It can be a delicate dance, and let's be honest, many times we clam up and feel uneasy in the face of such prospects. But good news! It doesn't *have* to be complicated! Receiving love can feel as simple as breathing. It is our logical brain that tends to make it complicated.

'A mind all logic is like a knife all blade. It makes the hand bleed that uses it.'

Rabindranath Tagore

Let me break it down for you in a simplified way:

1. Know Your Needs and Talk about Them

My husband and I have a very strong line of communication. We (almost) always discuss our needs with each other whenever we feel that need isn't being met. Thank *goodness* that discussion isn't utilized often, but it's there if we need it. Like a fire extinguisher.

It's important to be clear about what you need from a relationship. And I'm not talking about being demanding or expecting things from your partner, but about the basic requirements you need as a human being, like feeling safe, respected and connected. One study showed that being clear leads to a more satisfying relationship, with little chance of cheating and a much greater likelihood of commitment to each other.[55] Once you know what you need, it's crucial to have an open and honest conversation with your partner about it. Don't assume that they know what you need. People are so different from each other, and it's not fair to burden your partner with unspoken expectations.

2. Trust Your Partner

Trust is a big deal! I know it's hard to trust someone, especially if you've been hurt in the past. But if you want a healthy and loving relationship, you must trust your partner. Don't make them jump through hoops to prove themselves to you. Give them a chance to show you that they care about you and want to support your love and happiness. If they fail to step up to the plate, then it might be time to move on with love in your heart.

3. Keep It Simple and Selfless

When it comes to giving and receiving love, we tend to overcomplicate things. We get in our heads and lose touch with our hearts. It's important to give selflessly and receive graciously. Let the people in your life do nice things for you without feeling guilty or burdensome. Just like how you feel excited to make someone you love smile with a thoughtful gift, other people feel that same excitement when they can do something nice for you. So, let them! (Sometimes *you* are the recipient! And it can be that way on occasion.) Be sure to thank them with love and appreciation.

According to *Time* magazine, generosity (selflessness) is one of the key factors in maintaining a healthy relationship, and that goes both ways.[56] If your dog can figure out how to give and receive acts of kindness, I would think you can too. Another study published its findings about relationships and how better relationships are built on the foundations of give and take.[57] So you have to take a little sometimes. What's the harm? The giver will feel good about it, and so will you.

That's the recipe for a beautiful and loving relationship. It doesn't get easier than that.

Keys to Building Meaningful Connections

I'm a sociable person, so making friends is easier for me than it used to be. But the metamorphosis between 'acquaintance' and 'true friend' is a long one. That chrysalis could sit there for two months, maybe two years. It's completely unpredictable.

The more meaningful connections you have, the happier you will find yourself. Makes sense, right? When we have strong bonds with the people we love, our lives become infinitely better. We thrive when we have solid connections. And when something great happens to us, we can't wait to share it with our loved ones. That's because sharing happiness with others makes it even sweeter. So, let's connect and share the abundance of happiness we have with each other!

1. Respect the Opinions of Others

In my childhood, I shared with my grandfather the story of a girl in my class, whom we shall forever know as Pinki. She held a curious preference for leopards over pandas, a view I initially dismissed as silly. However, my wise grandfather taught me the value of respecting differing opinions. He revealed that our unique life experiences shape our views, making Pinki's preference valid, even if I couldn't fully understand it.

Now, it's essential to remember that there's no good or bad, only what serves us or what doesn't. Just because a particular way of thinking or belief doesn't work for us, it doesn't make someone else wrong or inferior. We're all humans, and we're all trying to do our best with the knowledge and skills we've acquired throughout our lives. It's crucial to respect other people's opinions and truths on this journey to happiness. As someone very wise said, 'Never miss to praise the good you see in people.'

2. Take Time Before You React

When it comes to communication, taking ego out of the equation can go a long way in building strong relationships. Think about the last time you argued with your significant other. You started out defending your side, but at some point, you began defending that position just because it was *yours* and not theirs. That point is where your ego jumped in. We should always take time to think before we react and speak. Impulsive reactions can lead to misunderstandings and cause harm to relationships.

3. Seek to Understand

Just like in the situation with Pinki, we must participate in perspective-taking when we disagree with someone; it's important to understand why they feel or think differently from us. Instead of enforcing our opinions, we should seek to understand their perspective. When we do that, we can still connect with them on a deeper level and maintain our relationship.

4. Stay in Control of Your Emotions

When Ashish or I get too emotional about our point of view in a disagreement, we walk away from each other. Maybe for twenty minutes, maybe an hour. Whatever the situation calls for. Sometimes we have to separate ourselves from the issue to gain perspective.

It's natural to face challenges and problems in relationships. Heck, we have challenges and problems with ourselves. In any case, it's important to stay in control of our emotions when we deal with situations. Listening to the other person with the intent to understand where they're coming from can help us solve conflicts and build stronger relationships.

> 'The single biggest problem in communication is the illusion it has taken place.'
>
> George Bernard Shaw[58]

There you go, friends! I know, loving and being loved is not always easy—but it is certainly worth the effort. Look, we've already learnt how to love ourselves; how much harder can loving someone else be? It's worth the effort. Remember that love is not just a feeling, it's a choice we make. It requires vulnerability, patience and communication. So, don't be afraid to open up to someone and show them your love. More importantly, don't forget to let them love you in return. It's important to understand that love is not about perfection, it's about acceptance and growth. So, keep learning, keep growing and keep loving, sweet peas—you've got this!

2

Communication

———

Building relationships requires an understanding of how to communicate with different individuals. Being attentive is extremely crucial. One way to strengthen our relationships is by creating rituals that allow us to spend quality time together and check in with each other regularly. And when it comes to communication, being open and attentive is of the utmost importance. *Frontiers* journal released a study correlating good communication with more successful, happier relationships.[59] Big surprise there.

It's easy to make mistakes and misunderstand each other. But we can avoid these misunderstandings with a simple approach: slow down, truly listen to others and clarify what they mean. Never assume—it's not a good colour on you. It might take a little extra effort, but it's worth it to prevent headaches and heartache down the road. We need to remember to make time for each other and be fully present in our interactions.

'Most misunderstandings in the world could be
avoided if people would simply take the time to ask,
"What else could this mean?"'

Shannon L. Alder

I can't tell you how many times I uttered X, yet Ashish perceived it as Y, leading to a comical cascade of miscommunication. However, we always find amusement in these episodes and engage in open conversations to untangle the confusion. I solemnly declare that I asked for cilantro, not parsley—precisely the one time I entrusted him with a trip to the grocery store.

Another important thing to keep in mind is that we should communicate not just when we're upset but also when we're happy. The *Frontiers* study pointed that one out too. It's so easy to forget to give compliments and express gratitude for the positive things in our relationships. But when we do, it inspires the other person to keep doing those positive things. Plus, when we do need to talk about something negative, the other person is more likely to be open and receptive if they feel appreciated and valued. So, let's make sure to communicate both the good and the bad in our relationships!

Barriers to Communication

We could probably fill up an entire book on the barriers to effective communication because the list is as endless as the credits after a three-hour movie. People who are committed to misunderstanding each other will find any excuse to disagree on things and argue, but that's only one way that communication between people gets misinterpreted, causing people to argue. Let's talk about the other barriers.

1. Physical Barriers

My husband knows how to come and find me (as I do him) to discuss anything that's on his mind. I *really* dislike shouting. It's probably my biggest pet peeve. If the person with whom you are struggling to communicate is a romantic partner, trying to yell at them across the house might not be the best way to talk to make them feel loved, seen or heard.

If you are trying to talk about something serious or talk intentionally about your day, it might be better to sit alongside your partner rather than across the table or while multitasking. 'Listening' while watching television is not listening.

Physical barriers are some of the easiest to solve because all you need is proximity! In today's times, the biggest problem arises physically when we try to communicate major issues over a device, be it phones, emails or SMS, because we can't express non-verbally through our tone and body language, which, as a result, affects our relationships. Even emojis don't do the trick. A study was conducted on this concept, and it found that people who actively partake in posting and interacting on the phone are less likely to understand the emotions behind text messages.

2. Perceptual Barriers

The trouble comes in when our own perception of ourselves or our partner gets in the way of communicating effectively. For example, for a very long time, a friend of mine insisted that she was a terrible communicator. Every time she found herself in a romantic relationship, she struggled to communicate her feelings and it didn't really go anywhere. It always comes back to the benefit of positive self-talk (and round and round and round we go).

One day, I asked her what would happen if she started saying the opposite—that she was a great communicator. I encouraged her to include this affirmation in her daily routine, like reading it out loud in the morning and setting it as an alarm on her phone. She really started believing that she was a phenomenal communicator. Poof, abracadabra, just like that!

Then she met a new guy and things just clicked. They started dating and seeing each other every day, and my friend was beaming with joy. When I asked her how things were going, she practically jumped up and down and told me that it was so much easier to communicate with her new partner. Sure, there were still some challenges, but for the most part, she was able to have a happy, healthy connection with him every single day. And it made her feel happier and more fulfilled in her relationship. So don't let negative perceptions hold you back: try to focus on the positive and believe in yourself! *We* believe in you; you might as well put in some effort too.

3. Emotional Barriers

Sometimes we may struggle with opening up and truly connecting with others because of emotional pain from the past. I'm pretty sure that getting hurt in a relationship is like a rite of passage. Sure, it feels tough, but it's important to realize that these emotional barriers can stop us from having fulfilling relationships.

A Stanford University study concluded that practising self-forgiveness can lead to better emotional and physical health. This outcome directly relates to more success and focus.[60] Maybe we need to work on forgiving others or ourselves and taking steps to heal those emotional wounds. Forgiveness and healing go hand in hand—just like you and your partner. I have never seen one done without the other.

It's not always easy, but it's worth it to try and move past those barriers and find a deeper connection with others. And sometimes, it's not just about us; maybe the other person also has some healing to do. Whatever the case may be, it's important to really dig deep into the trenches and see if old emotional wounds are holding you back from having a meaningful connection with other people. In the words of author M. Leighton, 'Happily ever after doesn't come easy. But for love, it's always worth the fight.' Don't let anything hold you back! You're a relationship ninja!

4. Natural Barriers

In our household, we always have flexible lines of communication open and ready. I never want to end up with parsley instead of cilantro again. Anyway, have you ever had a conversation with someone and left feeling like they completely misunderstood you? It happens all the time because everyone perceives life differently. We all have our own unique experiences that shape how we understand the world. That's why communication can be so tricky. But don't let that stop you from mastering communication skills. It's worth the sweat and labour because it can help you achieve your goals, solve problems and strengthen your relationships. Plus, being able to express yourself clearly can boost your confidence and sense of self-love.

According to therapist Sarah Epstein, 'Communication is what keeps couples on the same page and feeling like they are solving problems together rather than against one another.' More satisfaction leads to a stronger relationship, and a stronger relationship equals happiness.

'Communication works for those who work at it.'

John Powell

The Path to Better Communication

- *Listen More, Speak Less:* Remember, we have two ears and one mouth for a reason. Use it in that proportion. Mark Twain said, 'If God intended us to talk more than listen, he would have given us two mouths and one ear.' Isn't that basically what I just stated?

- *Stay Focused and Curious*: Listening isn't just about waiting for your turn to speak. Don't be that person.

Genuine curiosity allows you to understand others without the pressure of formulating a response. Listen to listen, not to reply. Trust me, it's worth it.

- *Don't Judge a Book by Its Cover*: You never know what someone's story is. Instead of making assumptions, choose kindness and be a good listener. As journalist Germany Kent wisely said, 'Be kind. We never know what people are going through. Give goodwill and mercy because one day your circumstances could change, and you may need it.' Let's start a kindness movement!

- *Show Empathy*: Sometimes, all a person needs is an empathetic ear. They just need to know that someone else is hearing them. Simply listening and offering an understanding nod for their suffering can be incredibly healing. Lend an ear and change a life.

- *Don't Make Assumptions*: Take the trouble to know the whole story. If someone says one thing, don't assume they mean something else. If in doubt, ask the person directly until you have clarity.

- *Focus on Your Body Language and Behaviour*: It's not what we say but how we say it that makes or breaks relations. Most problems arise because we are saying things in an incorrect way.

- *Be Clear*: Communicate what you need to the people around you. Don't expect them to understand your thoughts and feelings automatically. They are not mind-readers.

- *Don't Be Negative*: Never take silence to be the sign of a hidden and negative agenda. Who knows? They could be thinking about trains, cars or cricket. Wait for people to express themselves.

Communication can be challenging, but it is one of the most important skills that we can cultivate in our lives. From personal relationships to professional endeavours, effective communication is key to success and happiness. So, let's communicate with intention and empathy, and always work to connect with others in a positive and meaningful way. Together, we can break down these barriers and create a more connected and compassionate world! Storm the castle! Break down those walls!

'Communication is a skill that you can learn. It's like riding a bicycle or typing. If you're willing to work at it, you can rapidly improve the quality of every part of your life.'

Brian Tracy

3

Boundaries

~

Boundaries are like the rules we set for ourselves and our relationships, based on our values and self-worth. They're like a guidebook for our emotional and mental well-being, and crucial when it comes to maintaining healthy relationships. I've set a boundary of no yelling during arguments. Yelling really upsets me, and I think it's counterproductive to finding solutions to problems. So, whenever an argument starts to get heated, I ask that we take a break and come back to it later when we're both calmer. Use your 'inside voice', as my primary teacher used to say. This boundary is important to me because I believe conflicts can be resolved without resorting to emotional outbursts.

When people in a relationship start shouting, poor communication and lowered self-confidence—according to the *Wall Street Journal*—are often to blame.[61] Emotions are running wild, anger levels are heightened, and both parties start feeling exhausted and overwhelmed. As the fight intensifies, the volume increases.

Afterwards, both parties might apologize and feel guilty—so all's well that ends well, right? Wrong. The problem with this scenario is that there are harmful psychological effects at play. Basically, it weakens the relationship.

Why Do We Need Boundaries?

Well, they protect our time and energy from being wasted on things that don't bring us joy or happiness. They also prevent us from being treated like emotional doormats by others who might take advantage of our kindness. What did I tell you about letting people wipe their feet on you?

Ironically, my second biggest pet peeve/enforced boundary is when people wear shoes in the house. I can't stop thinking about the germs and microbes, not to mention the dirt they're spreading all over my nice, clean house. That's a personal thing. You might have your own such views.

It's common to be hesitant about setting and enforcing boundaries because we don't want to push away someone we love. But the truth is, anyone who truly loves and respects us will also respect our boundaries. And if they don't, well, maybe it's time to re-evaluate that relationship. 'Good fences make good neighbours.' Boundaries, people.

As Rumi once wrote, 'Set your life on fire. Seek those who fan your flames.' So, don't be afraid to set those boundaries and stick to them. It's an act of self-love and self-respect, and you deserve nothing less!

Tips for Healthy Boundaries

If setting boundaries is hard for you, you're not alone. I remember it took me a while to get the hang of it, too. I'm almost thirty, and I'm just getting there. It takes practice and can be especially tricky if you're used to being a people-pleaser, or you don't know where to start. Practice makes perfect. Keep at it!

1. Know What You Seek from a Relationship

Before I started dating Ashish, I had already written down my values, wants and needs in my journal. I always figured that if I wanted a real forever-relationship, I would need to know a few things about myself beforehand. I believed that blindly entering a relationship was a slaphappy way to go about it.

The first step towards building any healthy relationship is to understand yourself and your needs. Take out a piece of paper and start scribbling. Only when you know your values and worth can you give the best in your relationship and get the best out of it. Mind you, you don't have to enter every relationship with expectations of gaining something from it. The only thing you must seek is that your own values and ethics should never be affected. I always try to learn something in a relationship but never at the expense of my own values. It's just not worth compromising who I am.

2. Practise Healthy Communication

Just so you know, people won't automatically know your boundaries—they're not psychics! It's up to you to communicate what you're comfortable with and what you're not. When you express your boundaries, it can actually bring you closer to the people in your life. It's not about telling them they're wrong, it's about helping them understand what *you* need and giving them a chance to meet those needs. And because relationships are constantly changing, ebbing and flowing, you may have to readjust those boundaries sometimes. How do we do that? *Communication!*

Make sure to choose the correct place and time to explain and enforce your boundaries, and be compassionate in choosing your words. For example, it is ill-advised to do so just as they're sitting down to watch a football game or their favourite movie, or leaving to go hang out with friends.

Ultimately, setting and enforcing boundaries is a way to show yourself love and respect, and to create healthier, more fulfilling relationships with people. In a new relationship, this can be a difficult concept to execute. You don't want to offend the other person, and you're timid about approaching the topic. When I first met my husband, the 'not yelling' thing was extremely important to me, but I almost felt embarrassed about bringing it up. Now I'm super glad I did because our relationship is incredibly strong for it. Not that he was a yeller, to begin with, but I needed to be clear about this boundary. *No* relationship is worth compromising your values.

3. Stand up for Yourself

If someone continues to engage in behaviour or use language that you are not comfortable with, it can feel draining and disheartening to have the same conversations over and over. You must confront them about it and let them know that if this behaviour continues, you'll have to re-evaluate the relationship. No relationship should make you question your self-worth. If you don't feel respected, eventually, you won't respect yourself either.

'Respect yourself and others will respect you.'

Confucius

4. Take Firm Action

There have been some instances where my husband or I breached the boundaries we had set in ink many moons ago. It wasn't as if we meant to: it was the heat of the moment, we didn't listen carefully, etc. You choose your excuse. The injured party always points out the offence, and the offender always explains themselves and apologizes, and we happily make up. Okay, it doesn't always go as smooth as silk, but we make it work.

When you let people walk all over your boundaries, you're basically telling them that your boundaries don't really matter, that you're willing to change who you are and what you stand for just to make them happy. Changing your standards isn't fair to *you* one bit! Don't be wishy-washy. It's totally okay to say goodbye to people who don't respect your feelings and needs. It's not selfish or mean; it's an act of self-love.

Sure, it might be tough to say goodbye to those people who aren't meeting your needs at first. (After all, they probably have some wonderful qualities that you admire, or you wouldn't have taken part in a relationship with them in the first place.) But when you make room for the right people, it's a game-changer. Trust me, there are plenty of folks out there who will love and appreciate you just the way you are. So don't settle for less than you deserve!

5. Boundaries are Not for Control

Never forget your purpose in setting boundaries. They are set for your well-being, values and self-respect. They are there to help you understand what is allowed and what's not so that a relationship never drains you.

So always be mindful of not disrespecting or belittling your partner in the name of your boundaries. You have the right to stand your ground, but that doesn't give you the right to force your boundaries on anyone else. Remember, the other person is not your enemy. You're with them for a reason.

6. Accept and Respect Other People's Boundaries

This is a very important point. Many times, we make the mistake of considering ourselves as having the upper hand in a relationship. We feel that we are more important, or our wishes should be taken more seriously. To be in a happy relationship with anybody, the most essential thing is to consider and treat each other equally. You must be open to respect other people's boundaries, and if you feel you can't, you should discuss it right away and find a way forward.

How to Politely Confront a Boundary-Breaker

- Using 'I statements' can be a helpful approach. In fact, 'I statements' are *always* useful in communication or confrontation. This type of statement allows you to communicate your feelings and needs in a non-threatening way.

- For instance, instead of blaming the other person by saying, 'You always show up late to everything!' (which can make them feel attacked and go on the defensive), focus on your feelings and say, 'I feel rejected and disrespected when you are super late to an event that we have planned for weeks. Next time, please let me know if you will be late or let me know that you can't make it, and I will invite someone else.'

- Be specific about your problems. A little politeness will go a long way. This approach allows the other person to hear how their actions have affected you, without feeling attacked or blamed. It puts the emphasis on your feelings and needs, which helps them understand where you're coming from and gives them the opportunity to respect your boundaries.

- Using this framework can help you have constructive conversations with friends, family members and romantic partners where there's no yelling or shouting over the importance of boundaries. Arguing leads to regret, and regret is a waste of time.

A Guide to Framing an 'I Statement'

1. Start with 'I feel ...' to focus on your feelings to help the other person listen without feeling attacked.
2. Use 'when you ...' to clearly identify the boundary that was crossed and share how it made you feel.
3. Offer a solution by saying 'Next time, please ...' and work together to find a compromise that respects your boundaries as well as those of the other person. Remember that it's important to communicate your needs and collaborate to find a solution that works for both of you. It's all about that teamwork!

> 'If you're not a part of the solution, you're a part of the problem.'
>
> Eldrige Clever

Setting boundaries is important because it teaches others how to love and respect us. It's okay to have different needs and expectations, and it's important to communicate them to the people in your life. Whether it's a new friendship, relationship or a shift in dynamics within your family, having these conversations can lead to greater connection and understanding. If you're not sure that it's happening, some of the signs of people crossing your boundaries are:

- You're always putting their needs ahead of yours. If it's out of love, wonderful! But if you're constantly unhappy, reconsider.
- You're having to validate your boundaries time and time again.
- You've told them how much their crossing your boundaries makes you uncomfortable or upset, but they keep bulldozing right past anyway.
- They belittle your boundaries.
- They make you feel guilty over 'how much you've [supposedly] changed'.[62]

It's important to remember that it's only some of the people from those who cross our boundaries that don't care about us. The people who matter do care; sometimes they just may not understand what we need to feel respected and cared for. It's not about whether they care, it's about if they respect our feelings and opinions enough to take responsibility for their behaviour. If they don't, that's deliberate—there are no excuses.

At the end of the day, setting boundaries can be tough, but it leads to more peace and happiness in our lives. The people who truly care for us will respect our boundaries and do their best to meet our expectations. *These* are your peeps. This not only leads to happier relationships but also a happier life overall.

4

Differences and Letting Go

It's interesting. When you're dating someone, you get to know the person inside out. Their likes, their dislikes—it's as if you've been friends since birth. But then you move in with each other. That's a whole other story. It turns out that the person you're living with isn't the person you thought you knew! They are still charming, kind, beautiful, charismatic, loving … yeah, yeah, yeah. But there are eccentricities that you never knew about that you're about to discover like an avalanche. Did you know that they get mad when you accidentally leave the cap off the toothpaste? How about the thing where you have to push your chair in when leaving the table? These may seem like little oversights to you, but they're a big deal for them.

Relationships can be tough, am I right? We're all unique individuals with our own quirks and perspectives, and sometimes those differences can cause clashes. But that's just part of life, and we can't let those differences define our relationships. We need to deal with them sensibly and maturely, with empathy and understanding.

So, let's dive into some old-school ways to handle differences and disagreements in any relationship. Trust me, these tips have been tested by generations of wise folks, and they really work!

1. Separate the Problem from the Person

When we are angry or upset about something, it's essential to separate the problem from the person. Instead of attacking the person, focus on the issue and work towards solving it together. Remember, you and your partner/family are on the same side, and it's the problem that needs fixing.

> 'Let's not forget it's you and me vs the problem. Not you vs me.'
>
> Steve Maraboli

2. Avoid Reacting in Anger

It's important to give yourself some time to calm down and gather your thoughts before responding. As the saying goes, 'A hot head can only make things worse.'

> 'The greatest remedy for anger is delay.'
>
> Thomas Paine

3. Choose Your Words Wisely

Our words are powerful, and they can make or break relationships. It's crucial to choose words wisely and speak with kindness, even when we disagree. Stay focused on the problem at hand.

4. Don't Sweat the Small Stuff

Not everything needs to be fixed, and it's essential to remember: never sweat the small stuff. Petty arguments are not worth sacrificing a long-term relationship. Instead, focus on the bigger picture and happiness in the relationship. Besides, when you obsess over the small stuff, it takes a toll on your health. And we're all about being healthy these days, aren't we?

5. Ego Has No Place in Relationships

Our ego is not our true self, and It's crucial to leave our egos outside our relationships and have a humble and understanding approach.

> 'The ego says, "I shouldn't have to suffer," and that thought makes you suffer so much more.'
>
> Eckhart Tolle

6. Timing Is Everything

Maintaining our calm and composure during the right moment is critical. Live your life by the three Cs: calm, cool and collected. Instead of blaming others for their behaviour, focus on how you react to it. That gives you a choice in the matter.

7. Acceptance and Change

Sometimes we can't change a situation, and it's essential to accept it completely and readily. At other times we need to take action and change the situation. Regardless of the outcome, it's crucial to take responsibility for our choices and actions.

8. Responding to Unchangeable Situations

Life is full of surprises, and not all of them are pleasant. There are certain things in life that we cannot change no matter how hard we try. We might face situations where we feel helpless or powerless. However, what we can control is our response to these situations. We can choose to react with anger, frustration or despair, or we can travel down another road and respond in a better way. Choose wisely! An old Chinese proverb teaches us, 'The wise adapt themselves to circumstances, as water molds itself to the pitcher.'[63]

9. Being Sensitive in Relationships

Being sensitive means being aware of other people's feelings, thoughts and needs, and responding to them with empathy and understanding. It's about being able to put yourself in someone else's shoes and see things from their perspective. Figuratively. Don't literally slip into their shoes. That's odd behaviour, and it won't tell you anything. That said, a study was conducted that showed that spouses who are more empathetic in their communications have a lesser chance of showing negative support towards each other.[64] Not exactly ground-breaking but surely confirmational and therefore comforting.

When we deal with others sensitively, we show them that we value and respect them. We also create an environment of trust, where people feel safe to express themselves honestly and openly. But if we are insensitive, we risk permanently damaging our relationships, as the injured party may feel ignored, dismissed or disrespected. Our new mission is to uplift people! Making them feel smaller is a contradictory effort to that end.

Relationships require work, understanding and patience. We may not always agree with our loved ones, but we can always handle our differences and disagreements with kindness and empathy. Like the old souls we are.

'Love is not really a mystery. It is a process like anything else. A process that requires trust, effort, focus, and commitment by two willing partners.'

Elizabeth Bourgeret

Letting Go of Toxicity

I think back to that toxic friendship with Priyanka. I wrapped my arms around it as if it were indispensable for my survival. I believed that if I could hold on just a little bit longer, everything would work itself out. That wasn't the case. And I'm grateful for being wrong.

- Holding on to things we love can be brave, but letting go and moving forward can make us stronger. I know it's tough, but sometimes it's necessary to move on and focus on positivity.

- Letting go can be a scary prospect. What makes it so rough is you've invested so much time and effort into saving the relationship that it seems like a terrible waste to leave. Why give up a not-so-good thing? Because that's the only choice left.

- When we focus on the things we love and the people who support us, it's easier to find happiness again. It's important to make the decisions that are best for us, even if it means letting go of certain people and relationships.

- Remember, there's no right or wrong here—it's about what serves us and what doesn't. You know, like when you don't like the doughnut, but your friend does. It serves her, not you.

- If someone doesn't align with our values or continuously breaks our trust, it's time to let go. We shouldn't compromise our self-respect just to make a relationship work. As the late, great Aretha Franklin once sang, 'R-E-S-P-E-C-T!'

- Remember, when you let go of the negative things, you create space for positivity and for the right people to come into your life. When you're surrounded by like-minded individuals who are positive and inspiring, you'll be able to match their high energy and make the most of the connections you build.

A joint study between Wellesley University and the University of Kansas discovered that the age-old adage that 'opposites attract' is bogus. People seek out others like themselves on a primitive, psychological impulse. One of the study's leads, assistant professor of psychology at Wellesley, Angela Bahns, said, 'We're arguing that selecting similar others as relationship partners is extremely common—so common and so widespread on so many dimensions that it could be described as a psychological default.'[65] I'd say it's not so much a default as a perk!

Finding Balance

It's important to remember that letting go of toxic relationships doesn't mean abandoning your responsibilities or leaving someone behind just because it's difficult to take care of them. Assess each situation individually and make the best decision for yourself and those involved.

Sometimes, letting go may mean setting boundaries and communicating clearly about what you can and cannot do in a relationship. Other times, it may mean seeking outside help or support to better manage a difficult situation. Remember, seeking help is *brave*. Ultimately, it's about finding a balance between taking care of yourself and fulfilling your responsibilities to those you care about.

> 'Letting go doesn't mean that you don't care about someone anymore. It's just realizing that the only person you really have control over is yourself.'
>
> Deborah Reber

When to Let Go

- If they want you to change in a way that goes against your values, it's time to let them go. You should be allowed to be true to yourself, even if that means saying goodbye to someone else. At that point, leaving is nothing short of liberating.

- Actions speak louder than words. If someone's actions don't match up with what they're saying, it might be time to reassess the relationship, ASAP.

- When you realize that you're the only one putting in effort, it's time to let go. It's tough, but sometimes it's best for you to close the chapter on a one-sided relationship.

- If they keep breaking your trust, it's time to let go for your own mental well-being. Don't let your emotions cloud your judgement. Emotions are fleeting; listen to the squeaky voice of reason in your head.

- Respect is key in any relationship. If you feel disrespected, it's time to rethink the equation. Your self-respect should never be compromised.

- If you can't be open and honest about your feelings, it's time to let go. A relationship should be a safe space where you can share your thoughts and feelings. If you don't feel safe, it's time to skedaddle.

Remember, letting go is not easy, but it can be necessary for your own well-being and happiness. It's important to approach each situation with empathy and understanding, while also staying true to your own values and needs. Life is a journey full of crests and troughs, but with the right mindset and support, we can navigate it with strength and elegance.

'To let go does not mean to get rid of. To let go means to let be. When we let be with compassion, things come and go on their own.'

Jack Kornfield

5
Family

One of the quirkiest truths to grasp as a child (and let's be real, even as a grown-up) is that our parents are more than just our father and mother. Oh no, they are far more than the one-dimensional labels we bestowed upon them. In my youthful ignorance, I saw my parents as nothing more than mundane attic cleaners and potential knitters (though that's pure speculation on my part). Little did I know that they led lives separate from my brothers and me! They toiled away at work, indulged in gossip, sipped tea, volunteered and I'm certain embarked upon countless other adventures.

So let's talk about family—the foundation of our relationships and our identity. Our family members are the ones who knew us before we even knew ourselves. But sometimes, we tend to have preconceived notions about them and fail to understand them on a deeper level.

It's important to remember that no family is perfect, and, I reiterate, we are all unique individuals with different behaviours. It's important to accept our family members as human beings beyond our relationships with them. Yes, your mom and dad have lives outside of you as well. This will help us understand and deal with them better.

Speak Up

In our family, communication has always been mandatory. You *had to* talk to them, or they'd just show up wherever you were. I know that communicating with parents or family members can be tough due to our upbringing or other reasons. But it's essential to overcome our fears and express our feelings. Here's a little tip—if you're too shy to talk face to face, use other means, like writing a letter, sending a message or a voice note. And if that seems too difficult, reach out to a close family friend or relative who can talk to them on your behalf.

Believe me when I say that a family nurtured with love will always have your back, and they can be your biggest support system on this planet.

Simple Checklist for a Happier Home

1. Don't Take Your Family for Granted

We have a habit of taking our family members for granted because we know they won't leave us. But you can lead a happy life with your family only when you choose to be a part of the family every single day. Go on, join the circus that is your family.

I know our schedules and moods are not always the same, and sometimes we just want to be alone, or our job might need some additional attention (it happens to me all the time). When that does happen, it's okay; but we must clearly communicate it and try to make up for it when we have the time. These bonds are tied with true love, and that involves paying attention to their needs, being aware of their personal situation and making efforts to make their lives better, even if it's inconvenient for us.

2. Through Thick and Thin

In our teen and young adult years, we feel that our family is our biggest enemy. Just a fly buzzing around our heads. Always remember that everything and anything can fall apart, and the one relation constant in our life is family. They scold us, explain things to us, get angry or harsh, sometimes they even hurt us, but they never give up on us. Your career, money, fame—nothing and no one can give you that kind of security except for your family. I would do anything for my family.

3. Timing Is Everything

We tend to think that once we get this promotion or earn a certain amount of money, we will dedicate more time to the family or do something big for them. But remember, timing is everything. There may come a time when you're finally ready to deal with them, but it's too late. Don't miss any opportunity to be there for your family.

Also remember, there is a time for silence, a time to let go, a time to let your loved ones do things their way, a time to cheer them on for their successes, and a time to help them get back on track when things didn't work out like they thought they would. Never let your ego enter your home. No matter who you are to the outside world, to your family, you are just one of them.

4. Mind Your Words

Always be very careful of what you say. We can say something harsh and unkind in less than a second, but it can harm someone for years to come. Don't do this to your family, or anyone else for that matter. Be honest but also conscious about what you're saying and how you are saying it. Use uplifting, encouraging and inspiring words. That's what we do. We're uplifters!

5. Make Quality Time

Don't stick to just what's convenient for you. Remember that they are worth the extra effort. You will miss them when they are gone and the truth is one day, they *will* be gone; what's unfair about it is that we don't know when. Don't learn this lesson the hard way. The regret will kill you. Communicate regularly with them, express your love, have the hard conversations when necessary, share how you feel. Be there for them and let them do the same for you. A 2017 study found that a good relationship with family is important to reduce stress and be healthier.[66]

6. Practise Patience and Forgiveness

Never forget that your family only wants the best for you. Their approach might be wrong at times, but their intentions are always pure. You need to be patient and practise forgiveness when things go upside down. It can be hard at times but in the long run, it will be fruitful. If you can be patient enough to wait in the queue at Starbucks for that grande latte, you can be patient with your family.

When I first got married, it never occurred to me that blending lives and families with my husband could be so difficult! Learning the new ways that his family does things, how his mum cooks, how she likes the house clean 'her way', how they greet each other. It was a trip! Once I figured out this new dynamic, everything else was smooth sailing. Patience!

Toxic Family Members

This is a *hard* truth: even family members can be toxic. People can be toxic. Your family is made up of people. Ergo, your family members have the capability of being toxic. Simple deductive logic.

Having toxic family members is quite an ordeal to cope with. Believe me, I know. I have some toxic aunts, and they make it difficult to navigate through family matters. But we can't just toss a toxic family member aside without a second thought. We are responsible for their well-being, and we must study where this behaviour is coming from. Who are you to judge? Their toxicity might stem from an illness, depression or a lack of support in their lives. Here are some ways that can help you in dealing with a toxic member of your family:

- Just because their behaviour is toxic does not mean they don't love you or their intentions are wrong. They might be very caring and loving, but their needs might be hard for you to meet. And in such situations, it's perfectly okay to maintain your distance. Their toxicity might rub off. It could happen.

- Encourage them to seek professional help for their issues. Discuss it with your other family members if needed and go for family counselling.

- Be compassionate and try to understand their inner struggle. Show them that you're there to help whenever they need it. Believe that no situation is permanent, and they just might come out of their funk, leaving the two of you with the possibility of developing a good, healthy relationship.

- Don't take their toxic behaviour personally. Whatever negativity they throw your way is because of *their* nature, not because you're in the wrong. Simmer down. Here's the flip side: you aren't always correct. But if you *know* that what you're doing is the right thing, don't let their actions bring you down. Smile until your face hurts because you will proudly stand by your opinion.

- If your position mandates you to be around the toxic family member, don't forget to practise self-care. Live up to your duties wholeheartedly, but make sure to take breaks for yourself and practise mindfulness, meditation, prayers or hobbies that make you happy.

- Practise forgiveness towards them, for your own peace of mind. It might seem hard, but to live with hatred or negative feelings for someone is even harder.

'We must develop and maintain the capacity to forgive. He who is devoid of the power to forgive, is devoid of the power to love.'

Martin Luther King, Jr

- Don't shy away from seeking professional help for yourself if you feel their actions are affecting your mental health.

At the end of the day, family is what matters the most. They are the ones who will always have our back, no matter what. Sure, we may have disagreements and misunderstandings, but that's part of the human experience. What's important is that we make the effort to understand each other and work towards building a stronger and happier family bond. So, let's start by accepting our family members for who they are, communicating with them effectively and making cherished memories together. Because when all is said and done, it's the love and connection we have with our family that makes life truly worth living.

'I sustain myself with the love of family.'

Maya Angelou

6

Friendship

I n this chapter, let's dive into one of life's most fulfilling relationships: friendships.

I've been fortunate to cultivate extraordinary bonds with people that exceeded my expectations. Being showered with such profound love is an indescribable sensation. So I wholeheartedly urge you to venture forth and actively seek individuals who harmonize with your very being (now that you've acquired the knack!). Embrace the opportunity to forge genuine friendships that transcend fleeting whims and fanciful illusions.

'A man's friendships are one of the best measures of his worth.'

Charles Darwin

The idea that two or more individuals can come together, amidst a sea of billions, to form a bond that brings happiness, comfort and support—in ways that sometimes even our blood relatives cannot—never ceases to amaze me.

It's often said that friends are the family we choose for ourselves, and I couldn't agree more.

Friendship is an integral part of our lives, and it goes far beyond just having someone to hang out or share a laugh with. True friends offer emotional support, companionship and a sense of belonging that can help us navigate life's challenges and bring joy and fulfilment to our lives. They're the ones you can call at two o'clock in the morning because you feel like going out for pancakes. They celebrate our successes, share in our joys and offer comfort during difficult times. They are the people we turn to when we need guidance, encouragement or simply a listening ear.

What Is the Essence of a True Friend?

For me, a true friend is someone who accepts me for who I am, listens to me without any judgement, supports me through the twists and turns of life, and is always there for me when I need them the most. But most importantly, it is someone who helps me in my spiritual journey and makes sure I don't fall into the wrong trap. Or any trap, for that matter.

The most remarkable trait of a true friend is their willingness to intervene when they see us veering off the right path They accept us graciously, with all our flaws, but they also help us become better people. They can have that hard conversation with you, openly and confidently. Yes, those friends who won't blindly nod a yes to anything you say. They might let you buy a hideous pair of shoes but they will never let you stay in a toxic relationship or harm others. Be the Alfred to your Batman! Speak your truth, even when it's difficult.

> 'The only reward of virtue is virtue; the only way to have a friend is to be one.'
>
> Ralph Waldo Emerson

However, it's important to acknowledge that not all friendships are worth maintaining. Throughout my life, I have had to come to terms with letting go of toxic relationships that were doing me more harm than good. While it may not always be an easy decision, it is a necessary step towards safeguarding your well-being. It may sting for a while, but in the end, you'll be better for it.

Dealing with toxic friendships can be a challenging and complicated process, but it's crucial to recognize the warning signs and act as soon as you can. While it may be painful to let go of a once-close friend, prioritizing our own emotional health and safety is paramount.

- *Recognize the Signs:* Toxic friends are those who drain your energy, are negative or critical, unreliable or disrespectful. They may make you feel guilty or ashamed, put you down, or constantly need your attention. If a friend is causing you stress or making you feel worse after spending time with them, it is likely a toxic friendship. Get out while you can.

- *Set Boundaries:* This means being clear about what you are comfortable with and what you are not. For example, if a friend is constantly texting or calling you, let them know that you need some space and cannot always be available. If a friend is negative or critical, let them know that you do not want to engage in such conversations. *Forbes* magazine writer Vallori Thomas suggests that there's no need to describe what's going on in great detail—keep it simple. And whatever you do, don't start the blame game; it will surely catapult your discussion into an all-out lexical brawl. It's important to communicate your boundaries calmly and clearly and to stick to them.

- *Practise Self-Care:* Dealing with toxic friends can be emotionally draining, so it's important to prioritize self-care. This means taking time to recharge, whether it's through exercise, meditation or spending time with other supportive friends. Go read a good book. Knit something. Taking care of your mental and physical health will help you cope with the stress and negativity of a toxic friendship.

- *Limit Contact:* If setting boundaries is not enough, it may be necessary to limit contact with a toxic friend. This doesn't necessarily mean cutting them off completely, but it does mean reducing the amount of time you spend with them—chisel that limit in stone. If you feel guilty, remember that it's important to prioritize your mental health and well-being. You need to take care of yourself. You're the only 'you' that you have.

- *Seek Support:* Having a support system can help you traverse difficult situations and provide emotional support. There's strength in numbers! If you feel like you need professional help, consider reaching out to a therapist or counsellor.

Deal with toxic friends with compassion. Sometimes, toxic behaviour may be a sign that the friend is going through a difficult time, and *they* may need *our* support. During such times, it's important to be there for them, but we must also be mindful of our own emotional boundaries. Other times, it may be necessary to set concrete boundaries and limit contact. Whatever the case may be, it's important to communicate in a respectful manner with kindness and empathy.

Maintaining Friendships

Making and keeping good friends can be a challenging task, leading some to believe that the only time to make friends is during childhood or the teenage years. Why limit yourself? As someone who has found some of my closest friends in adulthood, I can attest that it's never too late to make meaningful connections at any stage of life.

While maintaining friendships can be challenging, especially as we get older and our lives become more hectic, there are ways to ensure that our relationships withstand the test of time.

1. Check In

Make time for each other. Even if you have a busy schedule, try to communicate regularly and spend time with your friends. It can be something as simple as a weekly phone call or text exchange, or a monthly brunch or dinner date. Keep that connection going.

2. Express Yourself

Your friends are no different than your partners: Don't expect them to be capable of figuring out what's going on in your head. Discuss your problems and concerns with them. And listen when they express their feelings too.

3. Practise Empathy and Understanding

Your friends may have different experiences and perspectives from your own, so it's important to practise empathy and understanding. Try to see things from their point of view and be supportive and encouraging.

> 'You should not judge; you should understand.'
>
> Ernest Hemingway

4. Be There

It is vital to be there for each other during tough times to offer support and encouragement. But it's also vital to be with them in happy times—happiness doubles when your friends are around. They're the family you've chosen, so be good to them.

5. Be Honest

It's imperative that you're honest and open with your friends. You should never just say something to be in their good books. Placating them only hurts the relationship over time. Be open to accepting feedback as well, when *you're* the one whose life has gone off track. Honesty can maintain and repair a good friendship.

6. Communicate Your Concerns

We are all human, and we all lack that personal brand of perfection we so desperately want to have. But our *relationships* can be made perfect by trying. Honesty and transparency are essential for maintaining healthy and meaningful friendships. If there are issues or concerns, address them directly and respectfully. True friendship only becomes stronger by facing challenges together.

My friendships have survived spats and squabbles over the years. The reason for that is the calm, open forum we share. We take care to understand each other's views and unravel any issues and never leave a conflict unresolved. With such honest communication, we will always be there for each other.

I encourage you to cherish your friends, to let them know how much they mean to you, and to never take their presence for granted. In a world where so much is uncertain and fleeting, true friendship is a persistent anchor that can help us weather any storm.

'Finding a loyal friend is as hard as finding a tear drop in the ocean! If you have them, cherish them!'

Unknown

Self-Study

Exercises

1. Identify one boundary you need to set in a relationship (such as not being available round-the-clock, not tolerating disrespectful behaviour, etc.). Communicate this boundary to the person in a respectful way.

2. Practise empathy by putting yourself in someone else's shoes. Think about a situation where you have disagreed with someone and try to see things from their perspective.

3. Reach out to a family member you haven't spoken to in a while and make plans to catch up.

4. Take a deep breath and let go of one thing that is causing you stress or anxiety. Visualize yourself releasing it and feel the weight lifted off your shoulders.

5. Write a thank-you note to a friend who has been supportive and kind. Let them know how much you appreciate them and their friendship.

Journalling Prompts

- Write about a time when miscommunication caused a problem in one of your relationships. What could you have done differently to communicate more effectively?

- Write about a time when someone crossed a boundary. How did you react? What did you learn from the experience?

- Write about a time when you had to let go of a relationship. How did you cope with the loss? What did you learn about yourself and your needs?

- Write about your family dynamics. What are some things that you appreciate about your family? What are some things that you find challenging?

- Write about a time when a friend supported you through a difficult time. How did their support make a difference to you?

PART 6
JOURNEYING INWARD

1

Detachment and Attachment

⸺

Have you ever felt stuck in a situation that made you feel hopeless and lost? Have you ever felt despair, depression or disheartenment weighing heavily on your shoulders? According to a UNICEF report that the *Economic Times Panache* covered, as of 2021, one in seven Indians feel depressed—and that only addresses the fifteen-to-twenty-four-year-old demographic.[67] Well, I'm here to tell you that there's a powerful spiritual principle that can help you overcome those feelings and find peace in any situation. It's called detachment.

During my upbringing, spiritual values played a significant role, shaping my perspective on attachment. As a result, the concept of attachment remained somewhat elusive to me as I wasn't encouraged to form strong attachments to worldly possessions (for the most part). I was taught that everything can be given and taken away, that nothing truly belongs to us.

Detachment is a valued teaching in many religions. It is the practice of letting go of our attachment to temporary things, whether it's material possessions, relationships or our own ego. It's about recognizing that everything in life is impermanent and learning to accept things as they are, without getting too committed to any one outcome or experience.

The Root of Human Suffering

Ego and attachment are the root causes of most human problems. In the Bhagavad Gita, Lord Krishna tells Arjuna that the ego is the cause of all suffering: 'From the ego comes attachment, and from attachment comes desire. From desire comes anger, and from anger comes delusion. From delusion comes the loss of memory, and from the loss of memory comes the destruction of discrimination.'

Jainism teaches that attachment arises from false beliefs and misconceptions about the nature of reality. It says that attachment arises from ignorance of the true nature of the self and the world, and from mistaking the impermanent for the permanent.

When we become too attached to our own desires and expectations, we start to feel lost and disconnected from the present moment. We may become overwhelmed by our own thoughts and emotions, leading to feelings of despair or depression.

'True detachment isn't separation from life but the absolute freedom within your mind to explore living.'

Ron. W. Rathbun

The Solution

I know you too are tired of being trapped in the endless cycle of suffering caused by ego and attachment. Well, good news! There is a solution! To overcome the ego and attachment, many spiritual traditions advocate the practice of acceptance and non-attachment.

- Acceptance means acknowledging and embracing the present moment as it is, without trying to change it or resist it. Non-attachment means not being overly attached to our desires, expectations or outcomes, and never clinging on to those ideas.
- We must remember that our efforts are within our control, but the results are ultimately not. Many religions teach that non-attachment is how you achieve nirvana, heaven, moksha—whatever you believe in.

By accepting that everything is as it is and cannot be any other way, we can find a sense of peace and neutrality towards adverse situations. We can put in our best efforts without becoming too emotionally invested in the outcome, recognizing that the result is ultimately out of our control. In the early stages of my marriage, I held on to specific expectations about how my relationship with my in-laws should unfold. I had a predetermined version in my mind, envisioning their behaviour and interactions with me. However, as I interacted with them, I realized that their way of expressing love and care didn't exactly align with my preconceived notions.

Initially, I felt a tinge of disappointment, questioning why things weren't going as I had imagined. It was a pivotal moment when I recognized the significance of detachment. I understood that clinging to my expectations only hindered my ability to fully appreciate and embrace the reality of our relationship.

By consciously detaching from my anticipated version, I opened myself up to a new perspective. I began to see the beauty in the uniqueness of our connection. I acknowledged that their expressions of love, though different from what I had pictured, were genuine and heartfelt.

Through detachment, I learnt to value and cherish the genuine care my in-laws showed me in their own distinct ways. It taught me that detaching from our preconceptions allows us to embrace the richness of reality, enabling deeper connections and fostering a sense of gratitude for the love and kindness that is present, even if it doesn't align precisely with our initial expectations.

The idea of letting go of what we cannot control and focusing on what we *can* control is also emphasized in stoicism, a philosophy that originated in ancient Greece. The stoic philosopher Epictetus wrote, 'Happiness and freedom begin with a clear understanding of one principle: Some things are within our control, and some things are not. It is only after you have faced up to this fundamental rule and learnt to distinguish between what you can and can't control that inner tranquillity and outer effectiveness become possible.'

It's important to note that detachment doesn't mean we become completely helpless and stop taking action. On the contrary, detachment allows us to act from a place of clarity and purpose, free from the weight of our own attachments and expectations.

Our emotions are temporary; joy, sorrow and excitement all fade away with time. Their impermanence causes us suffering, so we need to detach ourselves from their hold over us.

One of the key principles of detachment is to never become too attached to happiness or to have hatred towards pain. By being neutral towards both, we can cultivate a sense of equanimity and avoid getting too caught up in the highs and lows of life.

Another important aspect of detachment is to recognize that life is full of change and uncertainty. We can't control other people's actions or external events, but we can control our own reactions, opinions and thoughts. By focusing on what we can control, we can learn to let go of what we can't and find peace in any situation.

Now, I know what you might be thinking. 'Okay, but how do I actually detach?' It's easier said than done, right? Well, here are a few practical tips that can help:

- *Practise Mindfulness*: Remember, mindfulness is the art of being present and aware in the moment. It involves paying attention to your thoughts, feelings and physical sensations without judgement or attachment. By practising mindfulness, you can learn to observe your attachment to certain things and develop a greater sense of detachment.

- *Cultivate Gratitude*: When we focus on what we have rather than what we lack, we can reduce our attachment to and desire for material possessions and external circumstances. Take time each day to reflect on what you're grateful for. We've already discussed the physiological effects of gratitude; now you can see how it impacts your life in a more complete picture.

- *Let Go of Expectations*: When we have expectations for people, things or circumstances, we set ourselves up for disappointment and suffering. Practise letting go of your expectations and accepting reality as it is.

- *Seek Support*: Detachment can be a challenging practice, so it's important to seek support from others who understand and practise detachment. This could be a spiritual community, a close friend or family members with a similar mindset.

'If you expect nothing from somebody you are never disappointed.'

Sylvia Plath

Detachment is not a one-time event, but a lifelong practice. It may seem difficult at first, but it is a practice that can be mastered with time and dedication—and the rewards are immense.

Through the practice of non-attachment, we can cultivate a mindset of contentment, detachment and equanimity, and we will ultimately transcend the limitations of the material world. As the Bhagavad Gita says, 'One who has given up all desires, who lives free from attachment, ego, and false notions, attains peace.'

2

The Cycle of Desire and Suffering

‿

Are you caught up in a never-ending cycle of wanting and striving for more? Do you feel like you're constantly chasing material possessions and experiences, only to be left feeling unfulfilled and unsatisfied in the end? If so, you're not alone. You have a billion brethren to keep you company. It's a common experience in today's world, but it doesn't have to be this way.

I am not one who readily holds on to things or people. Well, I try not to. The problem is that I am very emotional, and therefore I occasionally do end up falling into the attachment trap.

The False Belief

The reason our desires are insatiable is because we have been taught to believe that external things can bring us happiness. We are bombarded with messages, from advertisements and society at large, that promise us happiness if we just give in and buy certain products or achieve high levels of success. But the truth is, material possessions and external experiences can only provide temporary and delusional happiness. True happiness comes from within, from a state of inner peace and wisdom.

The Consequences of Uncontrolled Desire

People tend to create a false sense of happiness and fulfilment. Unfortunately, this can only lead to discontentment, emotional turmoil and lack of spiritual growth. In turn, we find ourselves in an everlasting state of dissatisfaction. An increase in attachment leads to the disruption of inner poise and peace. In this cycle, we see ourselves stuck in bondage and bent on accumulating karma.

'The desire for sense-gratification is the root cause of all suffering.' This quote, from the Acharanga Sutra of Jainism, highlights how desires for sensory pleasures can lead to suffering and dissatisfaction.[68] This is because these desires can become insatiable, and the more we indulge them, the more we crave them. Just like you crave owning the latest model of a car or getting to be in the corner office. All material satisfaction is merely the starting point of a fresh struggle. There may also be a feeling of disappointment or dissatisfaction when you are unable to fulfil these desires, which can also lead to suffering.

The more we chase after our desires, the more we suffer. Desires are like chains that bind us to the material world. Only by breaking these chains can we attain liberation.

When I was first starting out, and before I had met my Guruji, I found myself armed with a lengthy catalogue of aspirations. Picture this: a grand list of around a hundred desires ranging from writing a bestselling novel, embarking on a global expedition, hobnobbing with famous people, acquiring idyllic beach and mountain homes—quite the comprehensive collection of aspirations, capturing both the whimsical and introspective facets of my youthful mind. Ah, the materialistic dreams of my fledgling self!

The more we pursue success, wealth or pleasure, the more we become trapped in their web. We become addicted to their temporary satisfaction and blind to their real cost: the price is everything you stand for.

Therefore, it is essential to learn to control our desires and cravings if we want to find true happiness.

Transforming Desires into Positive Pursuits

We can't completely eradicate our cravings but we can learn to direct them towards positive pursuits. Instead of denying or suppressing them, we can transform them into those with a higher purpose. We can use our desire for success to serve others and make a positive impact on the world. We can use our craving for love to connect with others and share our joy and kindness. Now, instead of aspiring to own multiple houses, I help those who are homeless. It's much more gratifying.

In the Kama Gita, Shri Krishna teaches King Yudhishthira about the nature of desire and how to overcome it. He says that when we are attached to our desires, we become enslaved by them, and they control our thoughts and actions. Desire can be a source of suffering, but it can also be a powerful force for spiritual growth when channelled in the right direction. He teaches that detachment is the key to overcoming desire and achieving inner peace.

By cultivating detachment and directing desires towards spiritual pursuits, we can overcome the cycle of suffering caused by attachment.

Practising Self-Discipline and Restraint

Since I started exploring my inner wants and needs with my Guruji, I realized that the only travelling I want to do is inside myself. Yes, I may travel occasionally but I don't place as much value on it. I still have a desire, but it's for inner growth. To break free from the cycle of desire and suffering, we need to practise self-discipline and restraint. We need to learn to say no to our impulses and temptations—just like with toxic people. In case you've forgotten how, it's an assertive 'No!' We need to develop the ability to delay gratification and choose what is truly beneficial for us. At the same time, we need to set priorities and focus on what really matters in life.

'The uncontrolled, undisciplined mind is, by nature, the opposite of knowledge-wisdom and happiness. Its nature is dissatisfaction.'

Lama Thubten Yeshe

Reflection and Action

Since ridding myself of those earthly desires, I've found that I'm in a calmer, safer state of happiness. You need to identify your own desires and cravings to start the process that will change your personal world. What are you truly seeking in life? How can you channel your energies towards more meaningful pursuits? By doing so, you may find that true happiness and fulfilment are closer than you could possibly imagine.

Remember, your desires do not have to control you. With practice and dedication, you can break free from the cycle of wanting and suffering and find lasting happiness within yourself.

3

Contentment: The Key to a Transcendent Life

When was the last time you felt content and at peace with yourself and the world around you? In our fast-paced and highly competitive world, it's easy to lose sight of what truly matters in life. Running around and trying to be better than the other person is *exhausting*! We often find ourselves chasing after transitory pleasures and material possessions, thinking that they will bring us happiness and contentment. But the truth is, real contentment comes from within. With my Guruji as my guiding light, I've sought only internal 'pleasures,' the kind that enhance my soul.

The ancient wisdom of the Bhagavad Gita says, 'A person who is not disturbed by the incessant flow of desires—that enter like rivers into the ocean which is ever being filled but is always still—can alone achieve peace, and not the man who strives to satisfy such desires.'[69] This statement reflects the essence of contentment: being satisfied with what we have, letting go of our desires, and accepting life as it comes. Just go with the flow: water flows down the path of least resistance. Go down the river, not against it.

The metaphor describes our desires flowing like rivers into an ocean that is always being filled, suggesting that desires are endless; they can never be fully satisfied. The key to inner peace lies in accepting this fact and learning to detach from our desires. Instead, we should focus on finding peace within ourselves, regardless of external circumstances.

> 'Each one has to find his peace from within. And peace to be real must be unaffected by outside circumstances.'
>
> Mahatma Gandhi

Equanimity

I used to allow myself to be upset by people who were unkind, uncaring or who wasted my time. They crept into my thoughts and often ruined my hours, days or weeks. It was an unproductive way of handling things. Since finding my spiritual guide, my mind is much more settled. I don't stress. Instead, I allow the thoughts to pass over me like air. Mindfulness. Look to the earth's elements; they often help to develop the answer.

- One of the keys to contentment is equanimity—staying cool and composed even in difficult circumstances. By now we all know that life can be full of ups and downs, and we can't control everything that happens to us. But what we can control is how we react to these situations. Things aren't so bad when we don't let them upset us.

- In the words of Marcus Aurelius, 'Very little is needed to make a happy life; it is all within yourself, in your way of thinking.' So, when faced with challenges, try to maintain your inner peace and remain calm. This will not only help you deal with situations better but also give you the strength to find solutions and move forward.

- Please note, equanimity is not just about keeping calm in difficult situations; it's also about not getting too carried away by happy moments. It's like having a mental superpower that helps you stay balanced and centred, no matter what life throws your way. It's like being a Jedi, but for your mind.

- When you practise equanimity, you learn to let go of attachments to both the good and bad things in life. The idea is to cultivate a balanced and stable state of mind that is not overly swayed by external circumstances, whether positive or negative. This can help us avoid the extremes of emotional highs and lows and maintain a more even-keeled perspective on life.

- In the end, equanimity can help you live a more peaceful and fulfilling life. So, embrace your inner Jedi and cultivate your mental superpower of equanimity!

Simplicity

Simplicity is the path towards a content and transcendent life. It means letting go of attachment to material possessions, status and recognition. Instead, we should focus on the things that truly matter, namely our relationships, our inner growth and our duty towards society.

Mahatma Gandhi said, 'Earth provides enough to satisfy every man's needs, but not every man's greed.' We must learn to be satisfied with what we have and live a simple life. We're turning 'simplicity' into the newest trending topic. This doesn't mean we should stop striving for our goals or pursuing our dreams. It means that we should find joy and contentment in the journey itself, rather than in the destination.

Focus on What You Can Control

These days, I tend to put more emphasis on the things that are within my power. Before that, I saw a pattern emerging. When I focused on the things I could control, I was at ease. When I focused on the things out of my control, I felt unsettled. I picked up on that pattern, and I decided to nix the things I couldn't control, immersing myself in the things I *could* control like a warm bath.

We only have control over our internal thought processes and our reaction to any situation. No fuss, no muss. So, don't mentally torture yourself about things that are not in your control. No matter how difficult a situation may be, focus on what you *can* control—your thoughts, your actions and your attitude.

As Epictetus said, 'We cannot choose our external circumstances, but we can always choose how we respond to them.' So, choose to respond with positivity and poise, and let go of things that are beyond your control.

Duties and Responsibilities

I have a close friend who truly embodies the essence of selflessness and responsibility. Her unwavering commitment to helping her elderly neighbours with their daily errands is nothing short of inspiring. What's even more remarkable is that she does all this without any desire for recognition or reward. It's a joy to see how her actions have cultivated strong bonds of trust and friendship within her community.

Observing my friend's approach to life has taught me the importance of staying true to one's duties and responsibilities, even when it may not be convenient or easy. I've come to realize that when we focus solely on fulfilling our obligations with sincerity and dedication, without any attachment to the outcome, we can create positive ripples that extend far beyond our own lives. It's a simple yet powerful reminder that by selflessly serving those around us, we can bring a sense of purpose and fulfilment to our own lives as well.

'The sage does not accumulate for himself. The more
he expends for others, the more he does possess
of his own.'

Lao Tzu

And remember, no effort ever goes to waste. Always try
your best to do the right thing, no matter how small your
step is, without being attached to the outcome. When we do
our best, we can be content with ourselves, regardless of the
result. Say it out loud: 'We don't *care* about the result! It's
the effort that counts!'

The Burden of Expectations

When I was a kid, I learnt not to be attached to my
expectations of how committed people would be in
friendships. As a teenager, I learnt not to be upset by the
revelation that, despite my expectations, my grades may
suffer if I take on too much at the same time. As an adult,
my expectations of being a perfect wife and mother were
obliterated with a burnt dinner and some first-time-mum
mistakes. Expectations are useless because they usually lead
to disappointment.

Whatever we think in our hearts and minds, we want it
to happen. And if we don't get it, we become sorrowful. So,
what we must realize is that what hurts us is not the behaviour
of people but our own expectations. Again, this means that
true happiness comes from within, not from external factors.

Contemplate Often

As part of my mindfulness journey, I've learnt to jump into the bottomless cavern of contemplation. Thinking, without reservation, about how I'm living my life now and how I'd like to live my life has really helped me grow as a wife, mother, daughter, friend and of course as a human being.

Contemplate often about your current and ideal state of relationships, duties and responsibilities towards everyone, and venture to make things better. This means taking the time to reflect on your actions, relationships and duties towards society. It means being mindful of your thoughts, words and actions and going out of your way to improve yourself.

When we take time to contemplate and reflect, we gain clarity and understanding. We find contentment in knowing that we are moving towards our ideal state of being. Research has shown, through new neuro-imaging advances, that when you are in a state of deep contemplation (such as prayer or while immersed in nature) or mindfulness, your brain lights up with physiological changes. There's a direct link between contemplative practices and 'positive psychological effects'.[70]

Tolerance and Dutifulness

I am both tolerant and dutiful in all aspects of my life now that I'm older. I obey my parents. I love and respect my husband. I adore and protect my baby. And I am hardworking and responsible at my job.

As they say, have tolerance power like ice and dutifulness like fire. This means being patient and persistent in difficult circumstances, while also being committed to responsibilities.

In Jainism, the principle of karma teaches us that our actions have consequences, and we must take responsibility for our own lives. By doing our best in every situation, we can find contentment in knowing that we are living up to our duties and responsibilities. And that makes us a stronger, more resilient version of ourselves.

In conclusion, contentment is the path towards a transcendent life. By following these principles, we can find peace and contentment within ourselves.

'True contentment is not having everything, but in being satisfied with everything you have.'

Oscar Wilde

I couldn't agree more. In addition, I believe that true contentment goes beyond being satisfied with what you have. What I've learnt in my spiritual journey is that it equals being satisfied and happy even when you don't have anything—when you honestly don't need anything to be happy.

4

The Truth about Happiness

So, here we are! On the last but most important chapter in this story of happiness. Throughout our journey, we have talked about various aspects of life, such as self-care, healing, relationships and the world around us. But, at the end of the day, what truly matters is the world inside us, the essence of our being—the soul. Immortal and eternal.

This is where my Guruji makes an appearance again. He has helped me better my soul with love, commitment, charity and dutifulness. I feel lighter since I began my journey inwards, and I suggest you do the same. Plummet into your grace and discover what your soul really needs to cleanse itself of. It's a long journey, so hold tight!

The Soul

Though we may focus on taking care of our physical body and our external environment, it is crucial to invest time and effort in nourishing the soul. Because the body will perish but the soul will stay—today, tomorrow and for the infinite days to come. And we all know that we're going to require more work for the longer journeys. No matter how much you take care of everything else, if you don't take care of your soul, it is all for nought. For it is the state of our soul that determines our true happiness.

And the main element of this journey is this human life, a precious gift. Because only this human birth has the power to make us reach the ultimate goal of our life—making our soul achieve total liberation, otherwise known as moksha.

The *Samayasāra*, an important Jain text, asserts that the only way to attain true peace and happiness is through the purification of the soul. This involves shedding the karmic impurities that weigh down the soul and prevent it from experiencing its true nature. So, we must focus on our soul if we want to achieve the purest form of happiness.[71]

How do we do that? Let me share some anecdotes to understand this concept. The journey towards spiritual growth and enlightenment is an inner journey. It requires us to dive deep within ourselves to understand the true nature of our being.

'Purity and simplicity are the two wings with which man soars above the earth and all temporary nature.'

Thomas Kempis

Spirituality: Nurturing the Soul

Spirituality is a way of life that involves connecting with our inner selves and transcending our ego. It involves cultivating a sense of inner peace, harmony and balance that helps us find happiness in everything we do. Spiritual practice is the foundation of our happiness. It becomes a guiding light in our hard times and keeps us grounded when we are flooded with joy.

Spiritual practice involves the cultivation of ahimsa (non-violence), satya (truthfulness) and aparigraha (detachment) from material desires through the practice of meditation and self-discipline. And the drive for this practice is gaining knowledge from scriptures and spiritual gurus. Whatever form it takes, the goal is the same: to connect with our divine nature and be enlightened with the true knowledge of the soul. Remember, spirituality is not limited to any particular religion or belief system but is a universal human experience.

Please stay away from the false belief that spirituality kills ambition and aspirations. If you take a good look at what it truly is, you'll see that it redirects us towards a higher purpose. It helps us see beyond our individual selves who are lost in the materialistic world, and work towards the greater good, the emancipation of the soul.

The Illusion of Freedom

I haven't reached a state of true freedom yet, and I'm not sure I ever will. I don't mean to sing the same old song, but I'm only human. While I'm free from (most) earthly desires, can I ever be sure that my soul is truly free? I try my best and that will have to do.

Epictetus had a few choice words on this subject: 'Freedom is the only worthy goal in life. It is won by disregarding things that lie beyond our control.' We often think that freedom means being able to do whatever we want and act on any of our impulses. However, in doing so, we become slaves to our minds and senses. True freedom is the ability to accept and enjoy the present moment, free from the past and future. It is a state of being detached from material possessions and desires. Inner freedom comes from spiritual practice, which helps us overcome external adversity and our innermost enemies.

> 'The only time a lazy man succeeds is when he tries to do nothing.'
>
> Evan Esar

What Goes Around Comes Around

Karma, the universal law of cause and effect, governs all our actions and their impact on our soul's path. Every action we take and every thought we think has a ripple effect that reverberates throughout the universe and shapes our destiny. I'm pretty sure we all know some version of the Bible verse '... for whatsoever a man soweth, that shall he also reap'.[72]

By accepting this truth and taking responsibility for our actions, we can break free from the cycle of karma and pave the way for our ultimate liberation. We must strive to act with detachment and composure, accepting whatever life brings us with grace and neutrality.

Dharma

The concept of karma can be a difficult one to accept, especially when faced with adversity or suffering. However, by aligning our actions with our dharma, we can live a life that is in harmony with the natural order of the universe and contribute to the greater good.

The Jain and Hindu translations of dharma are similar, in that it is a law for human virtues and propriety. It is a set of rules that detail how we should behave as human beings—an adherence to truth, generosity, being true to your vocation, amongst other things. Buddhism likens dharma to a universal truth, a sense of obligation to work, family and society as a whole.

However, don't make the mistake of equating dharma with religion. While its definitions include 'duty', 'righteousness' and 'virtue', it goes much deeper. Dharma is the ability to understand the rights and wrongs in life. It is a guiding principle that helps individuals lead a life that is in harmony with the universe and brings them closer to spiritual enlightenment—exactly where we're headed!

Contemplating the Soul

To achieve inner transformation, we must overcome not only external adversity but also our innermost enemies: laziness, lack of focus and the habits that distract us from or make us defer spiritual practice. It's hard to achieve a spiritual state when you're sitting on your couch working all day, probably still in your pyjamas. Contemplation is one way to help overcome these enemies. So, contemplate these thoughts as often as possible, as a soul:

- Where did I come from?
- Where am I now?
- Where will I go?
- Where must I go?

Our journey towards happiness is incomplete without nurturing our innermost selves, our souls. The soul is the hero of this story, and it is up to us to take care of it wisely. By nourishing our souls, we will achieve happiness not only in this lifetime but also in the infinite tomorrows to come.

The journey towards self-realization and spiritual growth requires constant effort, focus and dedication. It helps us connect with our inner selves, understand the purpose of our lives, and find peace and contentment. Let's pull out all the stops and embark on this journey to achieve our soul's highest potential.

Self-Study

Exercises

1. Identify one attachment you have that causes you stress or anxiety. This could be a person, possession or situation. Write down why you feel attached, and then come up with three reasons why detaching could be beneficial for you.

2. Identify a desire that you currently have. Write down why you feel it and what you think having it will bring you. Then, reflect on the potential downsides of fulfilling this desire. Are there any negative consequences that could come from getting what you want?

3. Take five minutes to sit quietly and focus on your breath. As thoughts arise, simply observe them and let them pass without judgement. After the five minutes are up, write down how you feel. Did this exercise bring you a sense of contentment or peace?

4. Take a few minutes to write down what happiness means to you. What does it look like? How does it feel? Then, reflect on whether your definition of happiness is based on external factors or internal ones.

Journalling Prompts

- Try writing about the last time you were upset with someone. Consider how you might have handled the situation better, with detachment from the situation.

- Reflect on a time when you were able to detach from something that was causing you pain or stress. How did it make you feel? What did you learn from the experience?

- Reflect on a time when you fulfilled a desire but still felt unsatisfied or unhappy. What did you learn from this experience? How can you apply this lesson to your current desires?

- Reflect on a time when you felt truly content. What was happening at that time? How can you cultivate that feeling of contentment now?

- Reflect on a time when you felt truly happy. What was happening at that time? How can you cultivate more moments like that?

The Journey Continues

Dear Seeker,

Congratulations on taking a big step in your journey towards happiness! I hope that the insights I shared have helped you understand what true happiness is and how you can cultivate it. Think of it like a tree that needs nourishing, nurturing and love.

Throughout this book, we have explored the idea that happiness is a state of mind rather than an exterior condition. We have learnt that our desires are boundless and our control over the world is limited, temporary and illusory. Like an ice lolly on a hot summer's day.

Seeking happiness outside of ourselves is tantamount to trying to fill a strainer with water. It is an impossible task that will only lead to disappointment and frustration. While material possessions, social status and other external factors can certainly contribute to our sense of well-being, true happiness comes from within.

One of the final things I want you all to take with you is the knowledge of knowing the difference between joy, pleasure and happiness.

When we talk about pleasure, we're usually referring to the immediate, sensory experience of something that feels good. Think of pleasure like a quick-fix, a Band-Aid that temporarily covers up a wound. You might feel good for a little while, but eventually, the wound will start to hurt again. Similarly, pleasure is often dependent on external circumstances, like eating your favourite food or going on a fun vacation. While these experiences might make us feel good for a bit, they are temporary and fleeting. Once the experience is over, the pleasure fades away too.

Joy, on the other hand, is more like a sustained sense of happiness. When we achieve a goal or accomplish something that we've been working towards, we often experience joy. This feeling can last longer than pleasure, but it's still dependent on external circumstances. Once we achieve that goal, the joy we feel might start to fade as we look for something new to pursue.

That's why true happiness is something entirely different. It's a deeper, more profound state of being that isn't dependent on external circumstances. It's the sense of peace and contentment that comes from living a life aligned with our values and purpose. It's about finding meaning and purpose in our lives and feeling satisfied by the things that we do.

Of course, this doesn't mean that we'll never experience negative emotions or difficult times. Life is chock-full of unpredictability, and there will be times when we feel overwhelmed or upset. It's important to acknowledge and process our feelings as they arise. But even in those moments, if we cultivate a sense of inner happiness, we can weather the storm and come out stronger on the other side.

So, how can you develop true happiness? The answer lies in focusing on the soul's permanent happiness and not getting lost in the world of temporary gratification. We know that the real nature of the soul is to be happy, and it is always searching for that happiness. By aligning your actions and thoughts with your soul's true nature, you can experience a lasting state of true happiness.

Again, this does not mean that you will never face problems or hard times. Life has peaks and valleys, and it is inevitable that you will face challenges along the way. However, by keeping your focus on your duties and your soul, these challenges will not harm you or affect your state of being.

As you close this book and embark on the next chapter of your life, remember that the journey towards happiness is not a one-time event but a lifelong process. It requires constant effort and attention, as well as a willingness to learn and grow. Remember to be patient and kind to yourself. Take each day as it comes and embrace the challenges and opportunities that come your way with an open heart and a positive attitude.

I encourage you to incorporate these insights into your life and continue your journey towards true happiness. May you find happiness in all that you do, and may your life be filled with love, laughter and meaning!

References

The detailed references pertaining to this book are available on the HarperCollins *Publishers* India website. Scan this QR code to access the same.

6 Jan 2024

What does living with integrity mean to me?
- Trying to be kind
- Being honest (this is different than transparency, protect my energy)
- honouring myself 1st, not someone else
- respecting my own boundaries

ABOUT THE AUTHOR

Savi Sharma Bagrecha is an author, educator, a content creator and mother based out of Surat, Gujarat. Through four novels that have sold over 700,000 copies, she has become India's highest-selling woman author. *The Happiness Story* is her first work of non-fiction through which she shares her learnings and experiences in search of true happiness.

Savi also runs a self-learning studio, Svadhyaya, which focuses on personalized, value- and emotion-based ways of learning and unlearning for kids and parents. Happily sharing her life with her husband and a two-year-old daughter, Savi finds immense joy in the embrace of her family.

Know more about her on www.savisharma.com or follow her journey on @storytellersavi on social media.

ALSO BY SAVI SHARMA

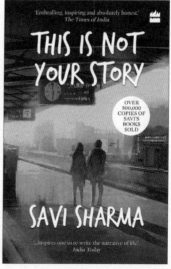

HarperCollins *Publishers* India

At HarperCollins India, we believe in telling the best stories and finding the widest readership for our books in every format possible. We started publishing in 1992; a great deal has changed since then, but what has remained constant is the passion with which our authors write their books, the love with which readers receive them, and the sheer joy and excitement that we as publishers feel in being a part of the publishing process.

Over the years, we've had the pleasure of publishing some of the finest writing from the subcontinent and around the world, including several award-winning titles and some of the biggest bestsellers in India's publishing history. But nothing has meant more to us than the fact that millions of people have read the books we published, and that somewhere, a book of ours might have made a difference.

As we look to the future, we go back to that one word— a word which has been a driving force for us all these years.

Read.

Harper
Collins

HARPER
PERENNIAL

HARPER
BUSINESS

HARPER
BLACK

हार्पर
हिन्दी

HarperCollins
Children'sBooks

HARPER
DESIGN

HARPER
VANTAGE

Harper
Sport